NICK'S SEAFOOD PAVILION, INC.
Yorktown, Virginia

NICK'S SEAFOOD PAVILION, INC.
Yorktown, Virginia

AMERICAN
HERITAGE

August, 1973 • Volume XXIV, Number 5

LETTER FROM THE EDITOR

Albemarle Street in London, just a few steps away from the noise and bustle of Piccadilly, is one of those quiet backwaters of good shops like Gieves, outfitter to the Royal Navy; its main landmark is that respectable and comfortable hostelry, Brown's Hotel. It is certainly no place to come suddenly upon a maiden in distress, let alone in deshabille. But there she was—and is, above; she was resting in the same position in a window of the Parker Gallery when we came by. The gallery is an emporium of paintings and old prints even more venerable than Goodspeed's in Boston or the Kennedy or the Old Print Shop in New York. There was no missing her, for the painting is over six feet wide.

It turned out, as we hastened within athirst for information, that the scene is the Battle of Trafalgar, October 21, 1805. Somewhere in the distance the victorious Lord Nelson is expiring, but in the foreground we have a shipwrecked lady named Jeanette, who has been deposited in the water in this distressing condition by the blowing up of the French ship of the line *Achille*. History, or at least solid legend, tells us that she was a stowaway, the young bride of a matelot. The sturdy British tars who are approaching eagerly to the rescue don't know all this yet, but everything ends decorously five days later, in true Gilbert and Sullivan style, when Jeanette's husband is rescued

too and they are reunited as prisoners of war.

While we were regretting inwardly that this scene really lay outside our American bailiwick we learned that the painter, a living Englishman named Leslie Wilcox, is in fact an enthusiast for the maritime history of our country. One thing led to another and resulted in a visit to Mr. Wilcox by one of our picture editors, Mary Dawn Earley, and the portfolio of his paintings beginning on page 20.

Collecting the pictures for this magazine, whether by such accidents as this one or by infinite pains and research, is one of the most enjoyable parts of our work. There is a kind of thrill in securing and publishing something for the first time, like the family pictures of Harriet and Calvin Stowe beginning on page 4. There are melancholy pleasures in sorting out the life of other times, with all its movement and activity, even when knowing that most of the places are altered beyond recognition, that the buildings no longer stand, and that so much of the humanity is dust. Pictures, of course, do bring back that past in some ways beyond the power of words; if you doubt it, study the Depression-era photographs on pages 41–54. Our sober colleagues on the historical quarterlies may confine their illustrations to footnotes and tables, but on this word-picture relationship we adhere to the well-known Chinese proverb.

—*Oliver Jensen*

2

AMERICAN HERITAGE

The Magazine of History

EDITOR
Oliver Jensen
ARTICLES EDITOR: E. M. Halliday
EXECUTIVE EDITOR: Nat Brandt
ASSOCIATE EDITOR: Barbara Klaw
ART DIRECTOR: Emma Landau
ASSISTANT EDITOR: Richard F. Snow
PICTURE EDITORS
Carla Davidson   Mary Dawn Earley
ASSISTANT: Devorah K. Cohen
COPY EDITOR
Joyce O'Connor
ASSOCIATE COPY EDITOR: Anne D. Steinhardt
EDITORIAL ASSISTANTS
Anne Anderson   Carolyn Jones

CONSULTING EDITOR: Joan Paterson Kerr
CONTRIBUTING EDITORS
Robert C. Alberts   Robert S. Gallagher
Richard M. Ketchum   Bernard A. Weisberger

ADVISORY BOARD
Carl Carmer   Eric F. Goldman
Gerald Carson   Louis C. Jones
Henry Steele Commager   Alvin M. Josephy, Jr.
Marshall B. Davidson   Howard H. Peckham
John A. Garraty   Francis S. Ronalds
S. K. Stevens

AMERICAN HERITAGE PUBLISHING CO., INC.
PRESIDENT AND PUBLISHER
Paul Gottlieb
EDITOR IN CHIEF
Joseph J. Thorndike
SENIOR EDITOR
Bruce Catton
EDITORIAL ART DIRECTOR
Murray Belsky

AMERICAN HERITAGE is published every two months by American Heritage Publishing Co., Inc.; editorial and executive offices, 1221 Ave. of the Americas, New York, N.Y. 10020. Treasurer, Marjorie C. Dyer; Secretary, John C. Taylor III. Correspondence about subscriptions should be sent to American Heritage Subscription Office, 383 West Center St., Marion, Ohio 43302. Single copies: $5. Annual subscriptions: $20 in U.S. and Canada; $21 elsewhere. A ten-year Index covering Volumes VI–XV is available at $5 and a five-year Index of Volumes XVI–XX at $5.

AMERICAN HERITAGE considers but assumes no responsibility for unsolicited materials; these require return postage. Title registered U.S. Patent Office. Second-class postage paid at New York, N.Y., and at additional mailing offices.

Sponsored by
American Association for State & Local History · Society of American Historians

COVER: In a detail from the picture at left Leslie Wilcox recreates one of the false starts of the *Mayflower* (center) on her voyage to the New World in 1620. The problem was her leaky, smaller companion, the *Speedwell* (left). After the first departure, from Southampton, she required this stop at Dartmouth. On the next start the *Speedwell* heeled badly and was left behind at Plymouth, whence, on September 6, the crowded *Mayflower* made her final departure. The picture appears by courtesy of the Parker Gallery of London; on page 18 begins a portfolio of paintings by Mr. Wilcox. Our back cover comes from the Long Island Auto Museum, Southampton, N.Y.

She had been brought up to make herself useful. And always it suited her.

As a child she had been known as Hattie. She had been cheerful but shy, prone to fantasies, playful, and quite pretty. After she became famous, she would describe herself this way: "To begin, then, I am a little bit of a woman,—somewhat more than forty, about as thin and dry as a pinch of snuff; never very much to look at in my best days, and looking like a used-up article now." She wasn't altogether serious when she wrote that, but the description was the one people would remember.

She was born in Litchfield, Connecticut—in a plain frame house that still stands—in 1811, when Lincoln

if she could have been born a boy.

As a child she had found most of his sermons about as intelligible as Choctaw, she wrote later, and never would she be at peace with his religion. But she loved him, and for all his gloomy talk of sin and damnation it is not hard to understand why. He was a powerful, assertive figure who had an almost fiendish zest for life—for hunting and fishing with his sons, for listening to all music, and for playing the violin, which he did badly. But could he only play what he heard inside him, he told them all, he could be another Paganini. Best of all he loved to go out and "snare souls," as he said. In a corner of the cellar he kept a pile of sand, and if his day was not enough to use him up, and stormy

said. "Then I won't do it!" And he didn't.

The happiest times in her childhood, Hattie would write later, were the days spent away from him, visiting an Aunt Harriet in Nutplains, Connecticut, in a house filled with books and pictures gathered by a seafaring uncle and a wonderful old Tory grandmother, who in private still said Episcopal prayers for the king and queen.

At twelve Hattie often wandered off from the noisy parsonage to lie on a green hillside and gaze straight into a solid blue sky and dream of Byron. One month she read *Ivanhoe* seven times.

In 1832, when Hattie had turned twenty-one, Lyman Beecher an-

THE UNEXPECTED MRS. STOWE

Harriet Beecher Stowe, an extraordinary member of an extraordinary family, always claimed that God wrote Uncle Tom's Cabin

was two years old and when Dolley Madison was in the White House. She was the seventh of the nine children Roxana Foote bore Lyman Beecher before being gathered to her reward, and she was such a worker, even when very small, that her preacher father liked to say he would gladly have given a hundred dollars

This previously unpublished daguerreotype of Harriet and Calvin Stowe is undated, but from their appearance it was probably made in the 1840's. Surrounding them, clockwise from top left: Simon Legree, Topsy, Eliza crossing the ice with Harry, and Uncle Tom and Eva—all illustrations from an 1899 edition of Uncle Tom's Cabin.

weather kept him from outdoor exercise, down he would go, shovel in hand, to sling sand about.

Sunday mornings he would come bounding along through the sunshine, late again for that appointed hour when weekly he brought down Calvinist thunder upon the heads of upright Litchfield people. He had a special wrath for drunkards and Unitarians, and he believed passionately in the Second Coming. But something in him made him shy away from the strictest tenet of his creed—total predestination—and its logic. Once when he had agreed to exchange pulpits with another pastor, he was told that the arrangement had been preordained. "Is that so?" he

By DAVID McCULLOUGH

swered the call to become the first president of the Lane Theological Seminary in Cincinnati. He packed up his children and a new wife and set off for what he called "the majestic West." A New Jerusalem was to be established on the banks of the Ohio. The family spirits were lifted; and crossing the Alleghenies, they all sang "Jubilee." A Philadelphia journal likened the exodus of the Reverend Mr. Beecher and his family to the migration of Jacob and his sons.

The following summer the Lane Theological Seminary's first (and at that time, only) professor, Calvin Ellis Stowe, a Biblical scholar and Bowdoin graduate, travelled west in the Beechers' wake. For all his learn-

MRS. STOWE—PAINTER

That Harriet Beecher Stowe was a painter—an engaging and talented one—is one of the unexpected facts about this small, slightly mousy, and intensely creative woman. Very little is known about her painting, beyond the fact that she apparently did not start doing it until she was middle-aged and that she neither signed nor dated her pictures, perhaps feeling that such formalities would be presumptuous. All of her known paintings have been donated by family descendants to the Stowe-Day Foundation in Hartford, Connecticut, and are on exhibit there. AMERICAN HERITAGE is pleased to publish, for the first time, some examples of her charming work.

The oval gouache on the opposite page shows Casco Bay, Maine. The sweet peas below it are painted in oils. Florida must have inspired the oranges at left, but nothing is known about the waterfall above.

Above, her house in Florida; below, her design for her china pattern

The snowy owl above is Mrs. Stowe's only known animal study.

These undated, unpublished daguerreotypes show the Stowe children—all except the baby who died—at various ages. Above, Frederick and Georgiana, the fourth- and fifth-born.

of old Puritans from his native Natick, all shadowy and dark blue in color, and one "very pleasant-looking human face" he called Harvey. They performed music for Calvin Stowe, and somehow or other they talked to him without making any sound at all, or so he said. He had no reluctance about discussing the subject, and there is no indication that any of his circle thought the less of him for it.

Still, the marriage proved difficult soon enough. Hattie became pregnant almost immediately, and just about then Calvin was asked by the state of Ohio to go to Prussia to study educational systems there. Professing a profound fear of the salt sea, he told her he would never see her again in

ing and devotion to the Almighty, Stowe was a very homely and peculiar worker in the vineyard.

He was accompanied by a beautiful young bride, Eliza, who soon became Hattie Beecher's best friend in Cincinnati but died not very long afterward. Apparently it was a shared grief over Eliza that brought Hattie and Calvin Stowe together. Years later, with some of the proceeds from *Uncle Tom's Cabin,* they would commission an artist to do a portrait of Eliza, and every year thereafter, on Eliza's birthday, the two of them would sit before the portrait and reminisce about Eliza's virtues.

The wedding took place in early January, 1836. What exactly she saw in him is a little hard to say. The night before the ceremony, trying to describe her emotions in a letter to a school friend, she confessed she felt "nothing at all." But Lord Byron had not appeared in Cincinnati. At twenty-four she may have felt she was getting on.

Calvin was thirty-three, but he seemed as old as her father. He was fluent in Greek, Latin, Hebrew,

French, Italian, German; he was an authority on education; he knew the Bible better than her father. Also, it is recorded, he had a grand sense of humor. But he was as fat and forgetful and fussy as an old woman. In the midst of a crisis, as she would soon discover, he had a bad habit of taking to his bed, and he had absolutely no "faculty," that Yankee virtue she defined simply as being the opposite of shiftlessness.

He also had an eye for pretty women, as he admitted to Hattie, and a taste for spirits, but these proclivities, it seems, never got him into any particular trouble.

But there was more. Calvin, from his boyhood until his dying day, was haunted by phantoms. They visited him most any time, but favored dusk. They appeared quite effortlessly out of the woodwork, the floor, or the furniture. There was a regular cast of characters, Calvin said, as real and familiar to him as anyone else he knew. Among his favorites were a giant Indian woman and a dark dwarf who between them carried a huge bull fiddle. There was a troupe

The eldest, twins Hattie and Eliza

this life. She insisted that he go, and had twin daughters while he was away. There was a third child two years later, then another, and another, and two more later on. A professor's wages were never enough, even when old Lyman could pay Calvin in full, which was seldom. Hattie's health began to fail. "She lived overmuch in her emotions," one son would explain years later.

"It is a dark, sloppy, rainy, muddy disagreeable day," she wrote once to Calvin when he was in Detroit attending a church convention. " . . . I am sick of the smell of sour milk, and sour meat, and sour everything, and then the clothes *will* not dry, and no wet thing does, and everything smells mouldy; and altogether I feel as if I never wanted to eat again."

She began going off on visits to relatives, leaving Calvin and the children behind. The visits grew longer. She went to the White Mountains, then to Brattleboro, Vermont, to try the water cure. The expenses were met by gifts from distant admirers of

Henry, the first son, who drowned

the family: the Stowes felt that the Lord had a hand in it. Hattie stayed on for nearly a year at Brattleboro, living on brown bread and milk, enduring the interminable sitz baths of one Dr. Wesselhoeft, and writing home exuberant letters about moonlight snowball fights. And no sooner did she return to the cluttered house

in Cincinnati than the professor hauled himself off to Brattleboro, there to stay even longer than she had. When a cholera epidemic broke out in Cincinnati and more than a hundred people a day were dying, she wrote to tell him to stay right where he was. She would manage.

In all they were separated a total of three years and more, and their letters back and forth speak of strong, troubled feelings. The hulking, clumsy Stowe, bearded, nearsighted, complained that she never folded his newspaper properly and that her letters of late were too uninteresting for him to read aloud to his friends. She in turn would run on about her own miseries. The house depressed her, she worried about money, she hated the climate in Cincinnati. She thought too much about death.

But she also told him, "There are a thousand favorite subjects on which I could talk with you better than anyone else. If you were not already my dearly loved husband I should certainly fall in love with you."

And Calvin would write to her when she was visiting her sister in Hartford, "And now my dear wife, I want you to come home as quick as you can. The fact is I cannot live without you and if we were not so prodigious poor I would come for you at once. There is no woman like you in this wide world."

In this same letter Calvin proclaimed to her—and apparently he was the first to do so—"My dear, you must be a literary woman. It is so written in the book of fate." He advised her to make all her plans accordingly, as though she had little else to do. "Get a good stock of health and brush up your mind," he declared. And he told her to drop her middle initial, *E* (for Elizabeth), from her name. "It only incumbers it and interferes with the flow and euphony." Instead: "Write yourself fully and always Harriet Beecher Stowe, which is a name euphonious, flowing, and full of meaning."

She had already written quite a little—temperance tracts, articles on keeping the Sabbath, New England "sketches," for which she drew heavily on Calvin's seemingly inexhaustible fund of childhood reminiscences. Once she had done an article about a slave. She had been selling these pieces to *Godey's Lady's Book* and one or two other magazines. She got two dollars a page on the average, which was more profitable than taking in boarders, she decided. But no one in the family, other than Calvin, had taken her writing very seriously.

She worked at the kitchen table, confusion all around, a baby in a clothes basket at her feet. She couldn't spell very well, and her punctuation would always be a puzzle for her publishers. She dreamed, she said in a letter to Calvin, of a place to work without "the constant falling of soot and coal dust on everything in the room."

Then in July of 1849 she was writing to tell him that their infant son Charley was dead of cholera. The summer before she had nearly died of it herself, with her father praying over her all through one terrible, sweltering night, the room alive with mosquitoes. She had been unable to do a thing for the child, she told Calvin. For almost a week she watched him

CONTINUED ON PAGE 76

Charles, the youngest

9

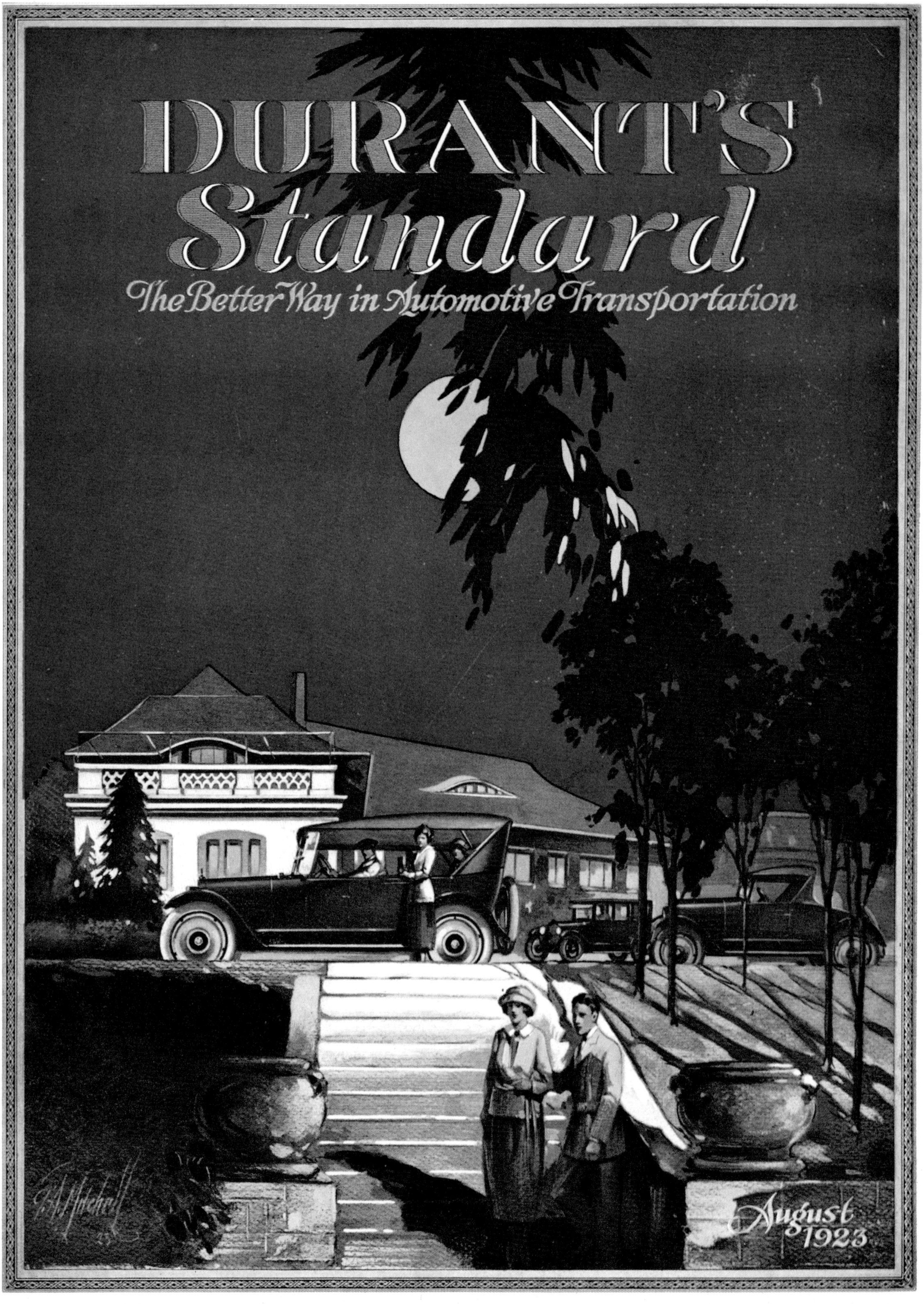

LONG ISLAND AUTO MUSEUM, SOUTHAMPTON

The General
of General Motors

On March 18, 1947, at 2:15 A.M., William Crapo Durant, founder of General Motors and Chevrolet and the "leading bull" in the great stock-market boom and crash of the late 1920's, died at his New York City apartment with his wife and nurse in attendance. His last fortune had evaporated in the Depression of the 1930's, and he had been an invalid for several years. People were already beginning to confuse him with Will Durant, the popular historian of philosophy. Within a few weeks Henry Ford, whose automotive career strikingly paralleled Durant's, was to die too—rich and famous but also ridiculed and despised. "Billy" Durant, on the other hand, left a public image that was clouded but untarnished. A eulogy in the Detroit *Free Press* said: "There was nothing of the ruthless pirate in Durant for all of his financial manipulations. Despite his fortunes and his power he was always a simple, human person, with a consciousness of the problems of the little fellow. . . . W. C. Durant typified the courage of American business, of free enterprise and initiative. If all of his principles are no longer acceptable, there are elements in his character that America badly needs today."

Those better acquainted with Durant knew he was not "a simple, human person." The man they remembered was a riddle. He projected a confusing, contradictory image to the world, and underlying the image were unfathomed depths. Durant had few intimate friends and did not encourage familiarity. The diminutive "Billy" was rarely used in his presence. Even to close associates he was "Mr. Durant," while subordinates referred to him as "the boss" or "the Man."

The short but indomitable creator of business empires was understandably dubbed Napoleonic by the press. This tag described aptly as well Durant's charismatic charm and his tendencies to be visionary, arbitrary, and impenetrable. One of the few bankers sympathetic to Durant probably sketched best his strengths and weaknesses: "Durant is a genius, and therefore not to be dealt with on the same basis as ordinary business men. In many respects he is a child in emotions, in temperament, and in mental balance, yet possessed of wonderful energy and ability along certain other well-defined lines." Even associates who liked and respected Durant as a person found this combination of traits difficult. Walter P. Chrysler, who began his automotive career at Buick, related: "I cannot hope to find words to express the charm of the man. . . . He could coax a bird right down out of a tree, I think. I remember the first time my wife and I entered his home. The walls were hung with magnificent tapestries. I had never experienced luxury to compare with Billy Durant's house. In five minutes he had me feeling as if I owned the place." But Chrysler resigned after only three years because he was frustrated by Durant's unpredictability and interference in Buick's operations. Chrysler knew they could never work together when Durant told him, "Walt, I believe in changing the policies just as often as my office door opens and closes."

Durant's dual personality was also noted by Alfred P. Sloan, Jr., who ultimately built Durant's brain child, General Motors, into the world's leading manufacturer of motor vehicles. Durant, said Sloan, had "a salesman's enthusiasm" and "tried to carry everything in his head. When some thought flashed through his mind he was disposed to act on it forthwith, and rarely troubled to consult with the man who had the real responsibility. . . . Yet even when this sort of interference struck as a lightning bolt into your own depart-

William C. Durant poses confidently with his latest automotive creation, the 1922 Star. With a price tag starting at only $348 it was meant to compete with the Model T Ford, but it did little better than the fancier Durant Standard, shown opposite in a setting intended to suggest that owners of the Durant would feel at home in an atmosphere of genteel affluence and leisure.

By JAMES J. FLINK *and* GLENN A. NIEMEYER

11

ment, you did not protest, because he was so sweet natured, so well intentioned. It was just Billy Durant's way. You accepted it, and perhaps liked it because you liked him."

In temperament Durant often seemed less like a businessman than a musician or an actor. He had a passion for classical music, especially opera, and he exhibited impeccable taste in furnishing Raymere, his show-place home at Deal, New Jersey. In contrast with his tendency to make business decisions involving millions of dollars on the spur of the moment, he spent hours personally designing the Buick and Chevrolet emblems. He was so moved by good theatre that he once had to leave abruptly after breaking into uncontrollable tears while watching Raymond Massey portray Lincoln.

At heart an actor himself, Durant scorned statistics, hard evidence, and logic in playing his entrepreneurial role. He relied instead on intuition and imagination, and his personal relationships were less cerebral than emotional. His strong drive to achieve was matched by an equally unquenchable need for approval and an intense loyalty to significant others. He protected himself by avoiding deep friendships while maintaining a surface affability to all and by being generous with money to the point of eccentricity. This kept most relationships formal and put them on a cash-in-advance, you-owe-me basis. Durant never dickered over price, and the salaries he paid were often exorbitant. Before Walter P. Chrysler could ask for fifty thousand dollars a year, Durant offered him five hundred thousand.

Incorruptible by money himself, Durant should have known that he could not buy true approval, loyalty, and affection. He was ultimately undone by trusting the yes men whose good will came cheap and then trying to protect the cronies who had gone along in his ventures.

In a lifetime that spanned the period from the outbreak of the Civil War to the beginnings of the post-World War II boom, Durant ultimately found what he sought from people only in his relationships with three adoring women: his mother, his daughter Margery, and his second wife, Catherine. The child is indeed the father of the man. And Durant's early experiences with a boy's normal male-role models were traumatic. The combination of a stern, prominent grandfather, a weak, irresponsible father, and an overdemanding, unsympathetic uncle left indelible scars on Durant's personality.

Billy Durant was born in Boston on December 8, 1861. His father, William Clark Durant, was a handsome, socially prominent banker at the time. But addictions to alcohol and stock speculation soon turned him into a drifter. He left one day on a fishing trip when Billy was seven and never returned. Billy was later to spend a small fortune in unsuccessful attempts to locate the father who deserted him so early in life.

The father's desertion drew Durant into a relationship with his mother that a psychoanalyst might well describe as oedipal. They were constant companions, bound to each other by mutual idolization. At the height of his success Durant would disrupt a busy schedule and travel days to spend a few hours with her. W. A. P. John, a reporter, found that Durant's most striking characteristic was "his love for his mother. Of the dozens with whom I have spoken concerning him, most have singled out that particular trait as most indicative of the man." With tears glistening in his eyes Durant confirmed for John, "Yes, that's all quite true. . . . She has always thought I was a wonderful boy. And I have tried not to disappoint her."

Rebecca Folger Crapo, the mother, could trace her ancestry back to the *Mayflower*. The Crapo family had made a fortune in shipbuilding and whaling by the time her father, Henry H. Crapo, moved from New Bedford, Massachusetts, to supervise personally the family lumbering operations in the frontier town of Flint, Michigan. Henry H. Crapo came to be reckoned one of Michigan's leading citizens, and in 1864 he was elected to a four-year term as governor of the state. The grandfather's achievements imposed a formidable burden on a boy in a culture that assumed one ought to do better than one's ancestors.

When Billy was nine years old, the Durants followed the Crapo family to Flint. Billy attended the Flint public schools, where he was a well-liked but mediocre student. A critical turning point in his life occurred when he was forced by the decision of his uncle to leave school at sixteen to take a job at his grandfather's mill at seventy-five cents a day. Bitter about the decision and determined to succeed in spite of it, Billy worked nights as a clerk in a local drugstore. This was followed by brief careers as a patent-medicine peddler and a cigar salesman. Durant then turned to selling insurance and real estate and undertook the management of the Flint water works. As a

Charles W. Nash, who started with Durant but left General Motors in 1916 to make his own cars, hands out checks to workers.

Above left: Louis Chevrolet in a 1911 model—the first of millions of cars to bear his name; right, Ransom E. Olds sits unmerrily at the wheel of an Oldsmobile already an antique when the picture was taken in 1921.

General Motors royalty in 1927, the post-Durant era: left to right, Lawrence P. Fisher (of "Bodies by Fisher" fame), Mrs. Fred J. Fisher, Alfred P. Sloan, John S. Haggerty, Mrs. Haggerty, and Fred J. Fisher

Inevitably, the booming automobile business brought famous industrialists and famous financiers together. Left, Walter P. Chrysler; above, Pierre S. du Pont with William S. Knudsen; right, John J. Raskob.

Early General Motors cars were mechanically somewhat unsophisticated, but their lineaments were ravishing. Could you have preserved either the 1917 Chevrolet Baby Grand or the 1928 Locomobile sport coupé (opposite) in amber, you would be rich today.

sideline he read gas meters. By the time he was twenty-five years old, William C. Durant had a reputation as one of Flint's most successful and enterprising young businessmen.

In 1885 Durant married Clara Pitt of Flint. But their temperaments proved to be irreconcilable, and despite Durant's continued success in business they were divorced in 1900. It was rumored that Durant sent Clara a present of two million dollars a few years later when she remarried—one of his characteristic attempts to smooth things over with money.

By the time of his divorce Durant was already a millionaire. His first fortune had humble origins. Shortly after his marriage to Clara he had acquired for fifty dollars the patent rights to a two-wheeled road cart, claimed by its inventor to have the riding qualities of a much more expensive four-wheeled carriage. Durant found a partner in

J. Dallas Dort, a hardware merchant. With two thousand dollars of borrowed money they formed the Flint Road Cart Company.

Their timing was perfect. A flourishing carriage-and-wagon industry was then developing in southern Michigan and northern Indiana because of the proximity of excellent hardwood forests and the rapidly growing midwestern market for vehicles. Since Durant and Dort were both salesmen who knew nothing about making buggies, they devoted their energies to sales and farmed out the production of their cart to a Flint carriage manufacturer. They bought the completed carts from him for eight dollars and sold them for $12.50. The profits from their first ten thousand vehicles were plowed back into the business, and the name of the firm was changed to the Durant-Dort Carriage Company.

Sales soon outstripped production. The partners decided that they would have to undertake the manufacture of their vehicle themselves. Fearful that the growth of horizontal trusts in ancillary industries would make components and raw materials hard to get at reasonable

14

prices, Durant and Dort purchased hardwood forests and set up specialized subsidiary companies to manufacture bodies, wheels, axles, upholstery, springs, varnish, and whip sockets.

By the turn of the century Durant-Dort had fourteen branch plants, hundreds of sales agencies, and annual sales of more than 150,000 vehicles. In a day when its competitors were mere order-taking assemblers of components, the company's emphasis upon aggressive sales techniques and its integrated manufacturing operations were major innovations in the carriage industry. Durant-Dort's bold conception of a mass market for low-priced vehicles and its attempt to blanket the market with a complete line of vehicles were other novel ideas that William C. Durant would apply to the manufacture of motor vehicles in a few years.

With his first million made and his first marriage on the rocks, by 1900 Durant had outgrown the challenges of Flint and the carriage industry. The days of the carriage-and-wagon industry were in fact numbered. Introduced into the United States in 1895, the automobile took America by storm. By 1900 the nation's leading bicycle manufacturer, the Pope Manufacturing Company of Hartford, Connecticut, had already switched over to the production of motor vehicles. And several leading firms in the carriage-and-wagon industry, including the Studebaker Manufacturing Company, the world's largest producer of horse-drawn vehicles, had begun experimental work with automobiles. In addition, hundreds of back-yard mechanics and small businessmen throughout the country were working on experimental cars and seeking financial support from local capitalists in order to enter the infant automobile industry. Southern Michigan was bound to be one of the hotbeds of such activity. It was not only a center for the production of carriages and wagons but also for stationary gasoline engines, which were widely used on midwestern farms.

One of the many Michiganders who attempted to enter the automobile business was David D. Buick, a Detroit manufacturer of plumbers' supplies and an eccentric inventor. He was soon deeply in debt, and his operation was bought by James H. Whiting, a Flint carriage-and-wagon

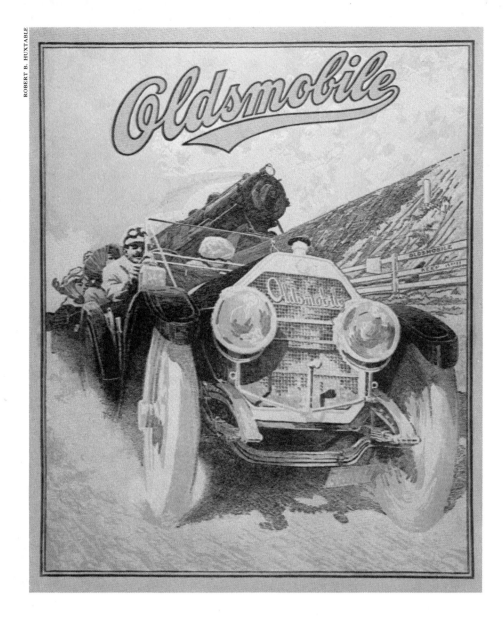

Then as now, speed and beauty were two of the automobile's chief selling points. The famous Oldsmobile ad at left hinted if it did not prove that an "Olds" could beat the Twentieth Century Limited, while the rather smug plug for the Oakland, opposite, almost implies that Michelangelo had a hand in its design. Note, however, that for the elegant model shown in the picture, the windshield was extra equipment.

manufacturer who had become alarmed about the potential inroads of the motor vehicle upon the market for horse-drawn vehicles. The Buick plant was moved to Flint. But Whiting was unable to get the floundering company off the ground. Only six Buicks were sold in 1903, sixteen in 1904. Whiting was under pressure from the Flint banking community, which had supported his venture, to find someone who could put Buick in the black. To the bankers and Whiting, William C. Durant seemed the perfect choice.

Durant had been unresponsive to earlier overtures to enter automobile manufacturing, and as late as 1902 he had forbidden his daughter Margery to ride in a car owned by a school friend's family on the ground that it was too dangerous. Probably he only considered Whiting's proposition because his mother had become a small Buick stockholder. Before committing himself, he personally put the two-cylinder Buick car through its paces on the worst terrain he could find. Satisfied that the product was a winner, he agreed to undertake the management of the Buick Motor Company on November 1, 1904.

Once in control at Buick, Durant moved with boldness and speed into the volume production of a reliable car in the intermediate price range. Buick's capital stock was increased from seventy-five thousand dollars to three hundred thousand the day he took over. On September 11, 1905, it was increased again to $1.5 million, and Durant is said to have sold nearly half a million dollars' worth of the new stock to his Flint neighbors in a single day. The Durant-Dort Carriage Company became a major source of capital for Buick, and Buick cars were exhibited in its salesrooms. Companies that had supplied Durant's carriage enterprise were shifted to automobile work. A national network of wholesale and retail distributors was established. In a few years the Buick car was substantially improved in quality for the price asked. Large assembly plants were built at Flint and at Jackson, Michigan, which turned those cities into boom towns reminiscent of western mining camps. Boarding houses rented beds to workers in shifts, and Buick was forced to become involved in planning housing developments for its employees.

CONTINUED ON PAGE 86

16

Oakland
"The Car with a Conscience"

Model 42, five-passenger
touring car, $1750.
Top and windshield extra.

True Mechanically—Truly Artistic

¶ In 1913 Oaklands beauty is given a new charm, luxury a new significance and individuality a new meaning.

¶ All that you care for in a motor car is found in the Oakland. All of the best and certain of the old and all that is safe and beautiful in the new, has found a place in the Oakland for 1913.

¶ Fours and Sixes, in a wide range of body designs. $1000 to $3000.

The Greyhound 6-60 — wheel base 130 inches, double drop frame, unit power plant, cone clutch, sliding gear transmission, full floating rear axle, demountable rims, "V" shaped German silver radiator, 10-inch upholstering, full nickel trimmings and equipped with the improved Delco electric lighting, starting and ignition system, $2,550. (Top and windshield extra.) There is mounted on this chassis four, five and seven passenger bodies and a raceabout for two. Price of all models the same.

Model 42 Chassis — 116-inch wheel base, double drop frame, unit power plant, cone clutch, sliding gear transmission, full floating rear axle, demountable rims, "V" shaped German silver radiator, 10 inch upholstering, full nickel trimmings and equipped with the improved

Delco electric starting, lighting and ignition systems, $1750. (Top and Windshield extra.) There is mounted on this chassis a five passenger body, a close coupled four passenger body and the famous Sociable Roadster (three passenger single seat). Price of all models the same. There is also built a smart four passenger coupe on this chassis selling for $2,500.

Model 35 Chassis — five passenger touring car, wheel base 112 inches, unit power plant, demountable rims, storage battery for electric lighting, nickel trimmings, $1075. We are also building on this chassis a three passenger Sociable Roadster, at $1,000. Model 35 will be equipped with electric lighting and ignition system and air starter at a nominal charge.

Write for Catalogue and booklets "What the Car With a Conscience Stands for" and "The Oakland Your Car for 1913"

OAKLAND MOTOR CAR COMPANY,
PONTIAC,   140 OAKLAND BOULEVARD   MICHIGAN.

The Seafaring Tradition

**An English artist recaptures
on canvas the American ships
that once ruled the seas**

The *Stag Hound* (left) was an impressive sight whenever she entered New York Harbor; she was so heavily sparred she could carry nearly eleven thousand yards of canvas. *Stag Hound* was the design of the eminent shipbuilder Donald McKay, his very first "California Clipper," the precursor of a style of sailing vessel that earned worldwide renown. The year she set out on her maiden voyage to San Francisco—1851—was a spectacular one for American seafarers. A sister clipper, the *Flying Cloud,* made a record run around Cape Horn to the West Coast, and the yacht *America* sailed around the Isle of Wight and won for us, permanently it seems, a prize ever after known as the America's Cup. "Speed," as one observer remarked, "was the spirit of the hour!"

The clipper ship represented the culmination of the era when the United States was the greatest mercantile sea power in the world. By no strange coincidence the first half of the nineteenth century also marked the coming of age of ship painting in America, for just as prosperous merchants watched the horizon for sight of sail, so artists trained their eyes toward the sea. To be sure, American painters had depicted ships before, but they had usually relegated them to background vignettes in portraits of successful traders or naval heroes to identify the source of the sitter's affluence or claim to fame. But as the Republic grew, experiencing the naval glories of the War of 1812 and the Tripolitan adventures as well as increased trade opportunities, the ship moved out of the background to become, along with harbor scenes, riverways, and seascapes, the proud focal point of a canvas. Whether she was a Navy frigate, a Salem brig, a Boston bark, a New Bedford whaler, or a New York clipper, the ship was the embodiment of adventure. The battles she fought, the storms she braved, the exotic ports she visited—all excited the popular imagination and the fascination of artists. To a great extent we know so much about this period of our history because the ship became a major theme for so many painters, including those as diverse in talent and style as Thomas Birch, Thomas Chambers, Michele Felice Corné, Robert Salmon, James Buttersworth, James Bard, and Edward Moran.

The days of sail are gone. The time when two warships would lock in deadly combat within sight and sound of each other really ended with the nineteenth century, despite a few minor exceptions. The era of America's dominance in sea trade is no more. American-flag passenger liners have almost disappeared, and none ply the Atlantic. And yet nothing can stir the blood like the sight of a great ship, her sails taut in the wind, her graceful bow plunging through a wave. Even if only a handful remain, most of them training ships, the memory is ever green. Artists and illustrators still portray the ship in her heyday—some lured to the theme by the continuing interest of art collectors, others by the subject matter itself. Of the latter, one painter who is notable is Leslie Wilcox, an Englishman and Honorable Secretary of the Royal Society of Marine Artists, whose *Stag Hound off Sandy Hook* appears here and whose other works are reproduced on the pages that follow. Wilcox painted his first American ship in 1930 after building a model from plans published in *Popular Science Monthly.* This stimulated his interest in American naval history, and after serving in the Royal Navy's camouflage branch during World War II, he seriously applied himself to ship portraiture. His library is extensive, filled with books on both our naval history and our naval architecture. His specialty is American clippers because, in his own words, "they were at the forefront of the merchantmen of their time, and I naturally wanted to paint some of the best-known vessels both for their achievement and their beauty." In future issues we hope to share with our readers the work of other living painters who help to maintain the American seafaring tradition.

The Oxford, *shown here leaving Liverpool, was one of a fleet of packets (ships that operated on regular schedules) owned by the famous Black Ball Line of New York, whose emblem flies from the topmost mast. The* Oxford *was launched in 1835, at a time when such vessels were comfortably outfitted for transatlantic voyagers willing to pay "thirty guineas, wines included." This*

*changed dramatically a decade later when Liverpool was the major port of embarkation for Irish emigration to the United States.
Spurred by the great famine of 1846, hundreds of thousands of Irish paid about twelve dollars each to sail on the packets, and conditions on board became wretched. Suffering from lack of water, poor ventilation, and disease, many died on the two-month crossing.*

Her small deck guns barking a salute, the David Brown *of* New York *(left) sets sail from San Francisco ahead of her rival, the* Romance of the Seas *of* Boston, *on the second leg of their famed maiden-voyage race to China. Both clippers were considered masterpieces
of design, and much money was bet on the contest. Although the* Romance *had left New York on December 16, 1853, three days behind*

the Brown, *she bested her, arriving on the West Coast ninety-six days later and a few hours before the* Brown. *They both sailed from San Francisco on March 31, 1854, and slipped into Hong Kong on the same day after a passage of forty-five days, but again the* Romance *won, by an hour. The* Brown *sank in the Atlantic in 1861. The* Romance *was lost at sea on a run from Hong Kong two years later.*

The John Wesley, *which was constructed in Searsport, Maine, in 1852, is surrounded by harbor craft as she departs from Venice past Santa Maria de la Salute. A mere 520 tons—as compared to clipper ships, which were fifteen hundred tons or more—the* John Wesley *was a typical New England trading bark, or "fruiter," as they were commonly called because of the cargo they brought from the Mediterra-*

nean. For many years Boston was the leading port in this trade. Her ships would leave home with "domestics"—that is, rum and Lowell cotton goods—sail to a southern port to pick up tobacco, then continue on to the West Indies for sugar and mahogany before heading across the Atlantic. They returned home with their cargo holds filled with oranges, lemons, raisins, nuts, olive oil, and wine.

The Savannah, *long heralded as the first steamship to cross the Atlantic, was built in 1818 as a full-rigged ship, but before she was completed, a Savannah, Georgia, shipping firm purchased her (and named her) and had her fitted with an engine, a smoke stack, and side paddle wheels. Actually, the* Savannah *never made the trip on steam alone because her boilers consumed more*

coal than she could carry. During her celebrated, but unprofitable, voyage between Savannah and Liverpool in the early summer of 1819, which took about four weeks, her engine was used for only about a hundred hours. A year later it was removed, and the Savannah was consigned to coastal trading until she was wrecked off Long Island in foul weather in the fall of 1821.

Historian by Serendipity

Bernard DeVoto lucubrates in his Cambridge study about 1950.

C. H. DYKEMAN

By WALLACE STEGNER

Bernard DeVoto, who died in 1955, was many things during his fifty-eight years—novelist, professor, editor, free-lance journalist, pamphleteer, and historian. In the 1940's and early 1950's he was best-known as the occupant of "The Easy Chair" in *Harper's*, from which he defended civil liberties, preached conservation, and asserted consumer rights with a vigor that endeared him to thousands as a giant-killer. His more permanent reputation rests on his histories: first *Mark Twain's America* (1932); then *The Year of Decision: 1846* (1943), *Across the Wide Missouri* (1947), and *The Course of Empire* (1952), the backward trilogy on the westward movement; and finally the condensed version of *The Journals of Lewis and Clark* (1953). *Across the Wide Missouri* won both a Pulitzer Prize and a Bancroft Prize; *The Course of Empire* won the National Book Award. It is as historian that DeVoto is a permanent part of American letters, and he was a historian by accident.

By accident, one says, and immediately draws back. Not accident—serendipity. He was a historian by the kind of inevitability that takes advantage of accidents. Also, he was a kind of historian many historians wish they could be, and others would not be if they could.

He told several stories about what he *intended* to be. One was that he set out to be a mineralogist but quit when he found that none of the perfect constructions of crystallography existed in nature. That story expressed his skepticism about all perfection but does not seem to have been true. Another of his stories was that he went to Harvard bent upon becoming a doctor (in one version a psychiatrist) but was diverted by World War I. It is true there was a spoiled M.D. in him, and true that he wrote much on psychiatry, especially in relation to literature, but there is no evidence that he ever aimed at medical school. When he came to Harvard in 1915 as a sophomore transfer from the University of Utah, he was already literary, and he stayed that way, despite some intense battles with the literary intellectuals, for the next forty years.

He wanted to be a "writer," by which he meant a novelist, and he did not fully abandon that ambition until after the publication of *Mountain Time* in 1947. His first three books were novels; six out of his first eight books, if we count those of his alter ego John August, were novels; in his lifetime, under several names, he wrote eleven novels and more than fifty short stories. Those facts had consequences upon his handling of history when he finally came to practice it, and they also indicate how far from history his intentions were. So does his training. He had no higher degrees. As a Harvard undergraduate he had a course in modern history with Harold Laski, a political scientist; one in the history of religion with George Foote Moore, a philosopher; and one in the history of science with L. J. Henderson, a chemist. That was it. His historiography was not by schooling but by inclination, imitation, invention, and carry-over from the art of fiction.

A historian without intention or academic training, he was also without institutional support. Though he taught from 1922 to 1927 at Northwestern and from 1929 to 1936 at Harvard, he taught in the English department in each case, at low rank and low pay, and at Harvard only part-time. He never had a sabbatical, he could count on no research aid, he never had a grant or a fellowship and never applied for one. And all the time he was writing history he never had an institutional salary but had to earn his living from the magazines. His bibliography contains nearly nine hundred items; only a small number of them are history. Except for one fairly concentrated decade, history was a spare-time occupation, too time-consuming to be much indulged.

And yet there was an inevitability awaiting its chance, an inclination needing to be satisfied. The inclination was partly geographical, the product of a boyhood in Utah's Wasatch Range, where he was born in 1897; partly pietistic, the result of being the grandson of a Mormon pioneer whose character and works he respected even while he repudiated the faith; and partly defensive, the professionally western pose of an outsider in Cambridge, Massachusetts, which he had to call effete even though he wanted to live nowhere else. He began reading western history as a homesick student, used it as material for journalistic essays and historical novels, and continued it for information with which to confute Van Wyck Brooks's theory that Mark Twain was a "spoiled artist." By preference he read firsthand accounts—the records of lived life were what caught his novelist's eye—and he focused on the West. Very early he was dazzled by the theme of the young nation spreading inevitably from sea to sea, carrying its vigor and its folkways with it. And he had grown up at the mouth of Weber Canyon, one of the great historical gateways of the West. When, later, he said he had always wanted to write about the Civil War but had been de-

terred by his own inadequacy and diverted to the second-best American theme, the westward movement, he was not quite candid, or was kidding himself. The Civil War was not his theme, though he knew and wrote a good deal about it. His theme was always the western one. Like Thoreau, westward he walked free.

When he came back to Cambridge in 1927, having resigned from Northwestern to live by writing, he had written no history except as fiction or popular-magazine articles. But in Cambridge he made or renewed acquaintance with a group of men all of whom, in individual ways, corroborated his addiction to the West and to social history, and influenced his way of reporting them.

One was L. J. Henderson, a passionate exponent of the inductive method. Another was Hans Zinsser, that bacteriologist of great integrity, low boiling point, and picturesque prejudices. Others were Kenneth Murdock and Perry Miller of the English department, who shared his interest in all things American. And there was a whole group of historians, especially Arthur Schlesinger, Sr., Samuel Eliot Morison, Fred Merk, and Paul Buck. All of them had a hand in his making. As he told a correspondent later, the way to become a historian was to go to an expert and be helpless. He did not add the corollaries that applied in his own case: go to a good library, say the Widener Memorial, and be industrious, and start some other kind of book—and history will come in by the side door.

His first excursion into history is listed in the libraries as literary criticism. It began in angry disagreement with Van Wyck Brooks's theory that Mark Twain was an artist thwarted and crippled by the Calvinism and cultural poverty of the frontier that bred him. In the course of his refutation DeVoto found it necessary to recreate the Missouri, Nevada, and San Francisco frontiers; to demonstrate that, far from being inhibiting, they had been stimulating, enlarging, full of excitement and wonder and the life of the senses, swarming with human types and charged with dynamism. Thus the book twisted in his hands. Schlesinger, Sr., was not far off in calling it the social history of Mark Twain, and he and Fred Merk knew what they were doing when they urged DeVoto to write a full social history of the frontier. The critics, too, were clear on what made *Mark Twain's America* important. Henry Seidel Canby spoke for many of them when he wished that DeVoto had thrown his stones in a pamphlet and written his book afterward; it was too good a book to be half spoiled by controversy.

It was an important book. It not only corrected some dubious deductions by Brooks; it remade Mark Twain criticism, and it made DeVoto a major authority on the frontier. But he set history aside, wrote another novel (*We Accept with Pleasure*, 1934), wrote serials, stories, and

This is one of the romantic but basically accurate paintings by Alfred Jacob Miller that stirred DeVoto's interest in the fur trade.

High in Wyoming's Wind River Range, trappers pause by the shore of a clear mountain lake, probably on their way to a rendezvous.

essays for the magazines, taught his way deeper into Harvard. But in 1936, being without higher degrees and being an interdepartmental maverick, a teacher of writing and contemporary literature whose major scholarly interest was outside the English department bounds, he found himself one of the first victims of President Conant's up-or-out policy. Wanting above all else to stay on at Harvard, he had to settle for the editorship of the *Saturday Review of Literature* and the role of public thinker in "The Easy Chair" at *Harper's*. From those two posts, which gave him unprecedented power in the literary world, he sniped at the literary Marxists for a lively but for him unsatisfying year and a half. In March, 1938, while retaining "The Easy Chair," he stepped out of the *Saturday Review* and into the curatorship of the Mark Twain papers. Both of those roles pointed directly to a continued career as a literary man.

And yet. The trussed and gagged historian in him struggled and bugged his eyes and groaned to speak. He had moved back to Cambridge, taking the Mark Twain papers along. Widener's western shelves were a daily temptation; his historian friends prodded him. As early as 1933 they had discussed a DeVoto trilogy with the whole westward movement as its subject, and he had written of it in letters to his historical conscience, Garrett Mattingly, once his colleague at Northwestern. It might have gone the way of all the fictional trilogies he planned, but it didn't. It worked in him as Manifest Destiny had worked in the Americans on their way west, as an urge below the level of consciousness, an inarticulate compulsion, an addiction that he neither quite named nor fully acknowledged. From very near the beginning he had focused on the year 1846 as the year when the "frontier bacillus" was most in evidence and when forces that had been operating in the West since before the Louisiana Purchase came to their climax: when Oregon came to compromise and Mexico to war, when the Wilmot Proviso settled the question of slavery in the territories, when the movement of covered wagons westward foretold that the Civil War, which was inevitable, would be won by the North. In conversation Paul Buck had begun to refer to 1846 as "the year of decision," and that phrase both expressed the evolving thesis of DeVoto's book and became its title.

In March, 1940, years after he had begun picking at the year 1846, DeVoto published "Anabasis in Buckskin," the story of the march of the Missouri Volunteers in the Mexican War; and in the fall of that year, crowding it into his prodigious work schedule between Easy Chairs and serials and magazine journalism and work on the Mark Twain papers, he started seriously to write what had been gathering in him for nearly eight years. On February 15, 1942, he wrote the last longhand page, had it ceremoniously signed by John Dos Passos and some other friends

gathered for a drink, and sent it off to Houghton Mifflin. Publication was held up, first by serialization in the *Atlantic* and then by a Book-of-the-Month Club selection, so that *The Year of Decision: 1846* was not published in book form until March, 1943. At once it was clear that here was a new kind of history—if, as some doubted, it was history at all.

In a half dozen essays and Easy Chairs beginning with "The Skeptical Biographer" in 1933, DeVoto had made assertions about the writing of history. One was that the literary should not be allowed to do it—they were temperamentally incapable of dealing with evidence, confused wish with fact, and characteristically used facts (as he said Van Wyck Brooks had done in writing about Mark Twain) to prove an a-priori thesis instead of drawing inductive conclusions from them. Another was that historians had too much ignored social history in favor of the political, economic, and metaphysical kinds. Another was that too many historians were narrow monographers, afraid of big subjects. Another was that they forgot the close relation between history and story and refused to dramatize; they habitually stopped on second base because in their view historians did not hit home runs. Another was that very few historians could write. Still another was that, even when possessed of the facts, historians had been trained to be timid in judgment. They mistakenly tried to make history a science; they suppressed the historian as artist.

The Year of Decision: 1846 flew in the face of all the conventions of academic history. It was not only narrative, it was a braid or weave of narratives of "some people who went West in 1846." "When you get a scene, play it," DeVoto advised Garrett Mattingly, and he practiced what he preached. He played the bitter Mormon exodus from Nauvoo, the ordeal of the Donner party, the march of the Missouri Volunteers, the adventures of Susan Magoffin on the Santa Fe Trail—all the stories of his fabulous year—for all they were worth. He strove to "realize the Far Western frontier experience . . . as personal experience" by using all the devices of evocation and vividness that he had learned as a novelist. He did not hesitate to judge. He called Zachary Taylor a lucky fool and John Charles Frémont a pompous publicity seeker; he made bold thumbnail sketches of James K. Polk, Brigham Young, Jim Bridger, a whole gallery. His positiveness did not please all historians. Frederic L. Paxson might remark that the book was "a brilliant job on the borderland common to the historian, the essayist, and the analyst," but DeVoto's old friend Arthur Schlesinger declared flatly that it was "not history," and many objected to the "inevitability" that was DeVoto's theme. "Inevitable," said Ralph Gabriel, "is a strong word."

But none denied the book's vigor, and the vigor came from the use of original and unorthodox techniques. Writ-

CONTINUED ON PAGE 92

THAT ZENITH
OF PRAIRIE
ARCHITECTURE
—The Soddy

*Pioneer farmers had neither wood
nor brick to build with, but
there sure was plenty of good earth*

By JOHN I. WHITE

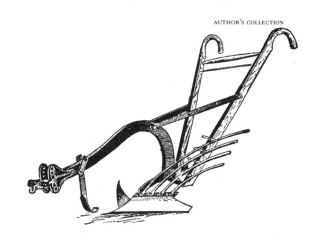

*Solomon D. Butcher roamed the Nebraska countryside in a horse-drawn "darkroom," taking over seven hundred photographs of sod houses
like the one above in Middle Loup, Custer County, in 1886. The grasshopper plow, top, was used to cut strips of sod from the soil.*

SOLOMON D. BUTCHER COLLECTION, NEBRASKA STATE HISTORICAL SOCIETY

"My father was one of the early home-steaders in Red Willow County, Nebraska. His homestead was located a few miles north of the Kansas line on high, flat divide land. . . . If he looked toward Kansas, what did he see? He saw nothing but sod. If he looked to the north, what did he see? He saw the sod. In all directions what did he see? He saw the sod. Consequently he used the sod to build his home."

It was as simple as that to Flora Dutcher when she wrote more than a half century later about her pioneer parent, a member of that hardy and independent breed who settled the western prairies in the decades following the passage of the Homestead Act of 1862. Father Dutcher's gift from Uncle Sam was strikingly similar to countless other claims in the Plains states—a hundred sixty lovely flat acres of free farmland, with not a tree in sight. There was nothing that one could use for building a log cabin, or a stone or brick one either. As far as the eye could see, in every direction, there was only the waving buffalo grass. However, the new settler had heard that a superior quality of turf is formed by the tough, matted roots of buffalo grass. So he took a few lessons in sod-house building from an experienced hand, borrowed or rented a special sod-breaking plow, rolled up his sleeves, spit on his hands, and went to work.

Before he could start his house, the homesteader first had to mow an acre or so of grass to get down to the sod. This done, he hitched his horses or oxen to an ingenious implement called a grasshopper plow, which gently turned over a uniform strip of sod from three to six inches thick and a foot or more wide. With a sharp spade he chopped these long strips

33

into convenient lengths for handling and hauled them to his building site.

Except that there was no mortar, the pieces of sod were laid much as if they had been oversize bricks. For the walls they almost always were laid with the grass side down. An entire first course was put in place, forming the outline of the house, then carefully levelled, with excess soil being pushed into the cracks, before the sec-

Jake Plum, his wife, and the family mules outside their sod house near Broken Bow, 1888
SOLOMON D. BUTCHER COLLECTION, NEBRASKA STATE HISTORICAL SOCIETY

ond course was laid. The second was staggered to cover the vertical seams in the first. In addition to keeping out the wind, a good tight wall discouraged unwanted visitors such as mice and snakes. Most walls were of double courses of sod and thus about thirty inches thick. Slightly moist sod was the easiest to work with and gave the best results.

Window and door frames were nailed together from old packing boxes or planking, provided the latter was available in the nearest town and the sodbuster had the wherewithal. The door was three or four boards nailed together with crosspieces.

Hinges more often than not were strips of old leather or canvas belting. The builder had to buy his glass windows or do without, using gunny sacks or heavily oiled paper until finances improved.

Planks or poles were placed above the window frames to keep the weight of the sod above from cracking hard-to-come-by glass. But since the house was bound to settle, a careful workman raised these supports several inches above the top of the window frame and filled the intervening space with wadding of some sort that would compress with the settling.

Interior walls usually were plastered and sometimes whitewashed as well, or papered with old newspapers. Most floors were of dirt, pounded hard. If there was any money around, it was wiser to spend it on the roof than on floorboards.

The roof was the big problem. For a small house a ridgepole was rested on the sod peaks of the two gable ends, and planks were run from it to the top of the front and back walls. If

tarpaper could be had, it was laid over the planks. Then, tarpaper or no, came a layer of sod, this time with the grass side up. As the sod, particularly when wet, placed a great deal of weight on the gable peaks, supporting posts often were placed under the ends of the ridgepole, either inside or outside the house.

Such a roof turned green with the spring rains, even sported wildflowers. But many a sod-house dweller has said it leaked like a sieve, especially a roof with only a slight pitch. When there was too much pitch, the sod had a tendency to slide off. Homesteaders who could afford shingles often added a layer of sod regardless. Along with being good insulation, both winter and summer, the sod weighed enough to keep the housetop from sailing across the prairie when a strong wind blew. Narrow eaves, or no eaves at all, also were considered good insurance against the wind.

A gable roof offered a great advantage over a hip or pyramidal roof when the homesteader's family grew and he needed to enlarge his house. He simply built another room at the end and extended the roof over it. Another method of expanding was to attach a low shed in the back and extend one side of the roof downward over it.

Apparently because planking was unavailable, in certain regions willow brush was incorporated into the roof, as was the case with the roof of the Dutchers' sod house in south-central Nebraska. "The ridgepole of my father's house was of cottonwood . . . rough hewn by hand," Flora Dutcher recalled in an article for the *Journal of Geography* in 1949. "It was supported by strong four-by-fours of lumber. The rafters were rough-cut poles laid from the ridgepole to the walls. These rafters were overlain with willow brush. This was in turn covered with carefully placed sod. All cracks were chinked with sod, and in time weathering rounded the roof surface to a smooth gentle oval which carried away the rain. Many times I have seen my father hoeing the weeds from the roof. The wind and birds carried the plant seeds up there. The growing roots opened the sod enough to carry trickles of water down through the roof and cause leaking . . . which was the bane of our lives."

There were times when the roof couldn't take it, as in the following account supplied by Mrs. Jane Shellhase for *Sod House Memories*, published in 1967 by the Sod House Society of Nebraska. Her parents built their soddy in 1878 near the Platte River in Phelps County.

"In June, after the folks were nicely situated in their new one-room soddy, it commenced to rain, and continued to rain for four days and nights. The roof was laid with willows, with sod on top of them, and naturally it began to leak.

"Father said, 'Let's get under the table.' So we did. The long ridgepole of the roof began to crack from the heavy weight of the wet sod and finally the roof caved in, with the pole resting on the table. We were buried beneath the sod and muck. Finally Father saw a patch of light and dug his way out."

Sod-house living included more inconveniences than a leaky roof. Bugs and mice not infrequently dropped from the ceiling into the soup or the baby's crib. A housewife could prevent this by tacking an old bed sheet to the underside of the roof.

An anonymous prairie poet once described additional perils:

How happy am I when I crawl into bed;
A rattlesnake hisses a tune at my head!
A gay little centipede, all without fear,
Crawls over my pillow and into my ear.

But it was not all bad. A soddy was cool in summer and easy to keep heated in winter, although because of the shortage of wood on the plains, fuel for the stove was likely to be tightly twisted hay, corncobs, or cow wood, the polite name for the dried

droppings of cattle or buffalo. A prairie fire that would quickly destroy a frame building had little effect on one made chiefly of earth. Furthermore, a dwelling with walls thirty inches thick was unlikely to be toppled by a howling blizzard. And provided one did not count the back-breaking labor involved, a soddy was cheap. Mrs. George H. Alexander of Omaha wrote in *Sod House Memories*

A soddy's thick walls are evident in this exhibit at the Old Court House, St. Louis.
NATIONAL PARK SERVICE

that in 1886 her grandfather built a 12-by-14-foot sod house in Lincoln County, Nebraska, for a total cost of $13.75, which went for lumber, a roll of tarpaper, and nails.

Poorly built soddies collapsed within a short period. Some that were built well lasted for generations. Thousands of rugged men and women spent much of their lives in them, brought their children into the world in them, died in them. Although given short shrift in books on American architecture, by helping to extend the frontier the humble soddy served a highly useful purpose. That so many people had the courage to

build and live in them is a marvellous demonstration of old-time American ingenuity and determination.

Nebraska has most of the survivors of the hundreds and hundreds of sod houses that once dotted the Great Plains. Professor Roger L. Welsch, a folklorist and the author of *Sod Walls: The Story of the Nebraska Sod House*, estimated that as late as 1970 between 150 and 200 families in the Corn-

husker State still lived homesteader-style—no doubt with tight roofs and certain other modern conveniences—behind the sturdy walls of antique soddies. The greatest concentration was in the vicinity of Broken Bow, Custer County. The newest soddy Welsch was able to find was one built in 1940—equipped with a shingled roof and a brick chimney—at Dunning in Blaine County.

John I. White, formerly an executive with a New Jersey publishing and map-making company, used to sing under the name the Lonesome Cowboy on the "Death Valley Days" radio program in the early 1930's.

The Burning of Chambersburg

By LIVA BAKER

In this imaginative engraving, based on a sketch by George Law, Rebel cavalrymen are depicted charging through Chambersburg.

Colonel William E. Peters stared at his commanding officer incredulously. Had he heard the order correctly? On whose authority was it given? he asked. Peters, thirty-five years old and a veteran of three years of fighting, had proved his bravery often enough; he had two wounds to show for it. But there were limits beyond which, even in war, he would not—or could not—go.

The general showed Peters the written order signed by his own superior. The colonel read it quickly. His response was unhesitating, calm, and resolute. No, he told the general, he would not obey. He would sooner break his sword and throw it away than make war on defenseless women and children.

July 30, 1864, was a breezeless, sultry day in Chambersburg, Pennsylvania, a fair-sized town made up mostly, during these war years, of women, children, and old men. Lying about twenty miles north of the Mason-Dixon line and never more than a night's ride from the Confed-

erate lines as the war raged up and down the Shenandoah Valley, Chambersburg had been raided, occupied, liberated, and reoccupied since the war had begun in April, 1861. Horses, wagons, and grain had been appropriated frequently and freely; warehouses holding government stores had been destroyed; merchants had had to spend a good deal of time and money shipping their goods to Philadelphia for safekeeping whenever occupation seemed imminent, then shipping them back again when the danger had passed; the town's womenfolk had nursed hundreds of wounded soldiers—both Confederate and Union—following the battles of Antietam and Gettysburg; and, of course, most of the eligible young men had been taken into the Union Army.

Nevertheless, Chambersburg's involvement in the war had been super-

ficial thus far. Hardship, yes, but not much more. The Confederate occupations had inflicted no casualties among the townspeople, and the town itself remained relatively intact. Indeed, with some rare exceptions, the soldiers' behavior on these previous occasions had been almost courtly; supplies had been requisitioned apologetically; the burning of government stores had been blamed on military necessity; the rebel soldiers had paid for the hats, socks, and gloves they had chosen in local

shops, and their officers had been entertained in the homes of prominent citizens. Confederate General Robert E. Lee himself, while camped just outside the town in Messersmith's woods on his way to Gettysburg the previous summer, had issued a general order reminding his troops that although they were in enemy country, "we make war only upon armed men" and "we cannot take vengeance for the wrongs our people have suffered without lowering ourselves in the eyes of all." Lee's order prohibited "unnecessary or wanton injury to private property" and promised arrest and summary punishment to all offenders.

But that was a year ago, a brighter day when, prior to the Battle of Gettysburg, the Confederates had marched into town triumphant, conquerors in enemy country, well able to afford magnanimity toward the conquered. Now, in the summer of 1864, that time of self-confidence and high spirits seemed dim and distant. Its resources, men, and morale almost exhausted, the Confederacy itself was only months from final defeat. In addition Lee, following his defeat at Gettysburg, had been soundly thrashed in the southern press for not leaving the country he had invaded in ruins; an informant had advised a Chambersburg resident: ". . . if ever the Confederates come again they will plunder and destroy; and my advice to you is, if ever you hear of their coming get everything out of their way that you can."

What was to happen in Chambersburg on the next to last day of July was the culmination of a series of escalating acts of retaliation for previous atrocities. Some months before, Major General David Hunter of the Union Army, operating in Virginia, had been harassed by bushwhackers and guerrillas who plundered wagon trains and assassinated Union soldiers. Once, in Charles Town, West Virginia, six of his soldiers had been found strapped to a fence, their

throats cut from ear to ear. Defenseless against the marauders, who posed as farmers and tradesmen by day and conducted their deadly forays by night, General Hunter distributed through the Valley of Virginia a circular in May, 1864, threatening retribution: ". . . for every train fired upon, or soldier of the Union wounded or assassinated by bushwhackers in any neighborhood within the reach of my command, the houses and other property of every secession sympathizer residing within a circuit of five miles from the place of the outrage, shall be destroyed by fire. . . ." As good as his word, by July, 1864, Hunter had burned, with particular savagery, the homes of several prominent Virginians and the Virginia Military Institute. As the guerrilla tactics of the Confederates had invited Hunter's retaliation with an increase in ferocity, Hunter's own escalation evoked a similar response.

Tough, tobacco-chewing Lieutenant General Jubal Anderson Early of the Confederate Army was not one to shrink from such a task. He himself had pursued Hunter through the Valley of Virginia and had witnessed "evidence of the destruction wantonly committed by [Hunter's] troops under his orders." Camped near Martinsburg, West Virginia, following his attack on Washington itself in mid-July, Early heard details of Hunter's most recent outrages in Virginia. He decided, Early said, that "it was time to try and stop this mode of warfare by some act of retaliation."

He ordered Brigadier General John McCausland, with his own cavalry brigade plus that of Brigadier General Bradley T. Johnson and a battery of artillery, to march on Chambersburg, to demand $100,000 in gold or $500,000 in greenbacks as compensation for three specific houses that Hunter's Union troops had burned. "In default of the payment of this money," Early's written

Left: General John McCausland, who led the raid on Chambersburg. Right: Colonel William Peters, who refused orders to burn the town. These are postwar photographs.

order declared, the town "is directed to be laid in ashes in retaliation for the burning of said houses, and other houses of citizens of Virginia by Federal authorities." Early had no particular grudge against Chambersburg; the town was selected, he later wrote, "because it was the only one of any consequence accessible to my troops, and *for no other reason.*"

Marching day and night, snatching what little sleep they could on horseback, General McCausland and his two cavalry brigades reached the outskirts of Chambersburg about three o'clock on the morning of Saturday, July 30. Colonel William Peters and his 21st Virginia Cavalry were among the advance forces. Resistance had been slight—a small force of Federal cavalry at Clear Spring had been driven off, another small force at Mercersburg also routed. At the fringe of Chambersburg a small unit of Union soldiers with one piece of artillery held the Confederates in check for about two hours. When daybreak disclosed the relative sizes of the two forces—twenty-six hundred Confederates to a hundred Union troops—the Northerners retreated through the town, "being careful," a Union officer reported later, "not to fire a shot within its limits in order that there should be no excuse for firing buildings or committing any barbarities upon the people."

The main part of the two Confederate brigades formed a battle line on hills commanding the town. The artillery was brought up, and three shells were fired into the town, inflicting neither casualties nor damage. When the shots were not answered, small squads of skirmishers immediately but cautiously advanced on foot through the alleys and streets of Chambersburg.

The streets clear, Colonel Peters was ordered to follow with his 21st Virginia Cavalry. Still unaware of the purpose of the raid, Peters obeyed quickly and efficiently. More cavalry detachments followed. By 6 A.M. Chambersburg had been occupied once again by the enemy, some five hundred of them, including the commanding general, John McCausland. The rest of the Confederate force remained camped outside the town.

Accounts of what happened next differ considerably in their details, because, no doubt, of the confusion, the noise, and the perspectives of the various people involved. McCausland's account is as reliable as any for the general outline of events:

I at once went into the city with my staff and requested some of the citizens to inform the city authorities that I wanted to see them. I also sent my staff through the town to locate the proper officials and inform them that I had a proclamation for their consideration. Not one could be found. I then directed the proclamation to be read to as many citizens as were near me, and asked them to hunt up their town officers, informing them I would wait until they could either find the proper authorities, or by consultation among themselves, determine what they would do. Finally, I informed them that I would wait six hours, and if they would then comply with the requirements [pay the ransom of $100,000 in gold or $500,000 in greenbacks], their town would be safe; but if not, it would be destroyed, in accordance with my orders from General Early.

McCausland's account omits any description of the behavior of his troops, behavior that Chambersburg residents later testified was barbarous from the moment the Confederates entered the town. According to witnesses, plunder began immediately at Mr. Paxton's shoe and hat store, followed by looting at liquor stores and in private homes. Residents were stopped on the streets at pistol point and divested of watches, purses, and clothing.

Nevertheless, the ransom was not paid. Some townspeople were willing to pay it; others were not. Some laughed at the demand, incredulous that the Southerners, whom they had known previously as the politest of enemies, would actually carry out their threat to burn the town. Some believed Federal forces were near and would protect them at the last moment—a faith that proved unfounded. Others protested that there was not that much money in the town, for upon learning of the Confederate approach the previous day, the bankers had discreetly fled, taking the money with them. Still others simply defied the invaders, saying they would not pay five cents even if they had it.

How long McCausland gave the townspeople before he ordered the town burned is a matter of dispute. The general claimed he waited the promised six hours; other reports set the firing time at two to four hours; one witness claimed the smoke was rising even while the general was negotiating with Chambersburg officials. In any case, the ransom was not forthcoming, and McCausland ordered his men to burn the town.

Colonel Peters was directed to move his men to the courthouse, arm them with torches, and fire the town. Peters, according to one Confederate military historian, was a man of "imperturbable courage. He couldn't be shaken. Earthquakes, tornadoes, electric storms couldn't move him. He would have stopped and asked, 'What next?' if the earth were opening beneath him and the mountains falling on him." He had joined the Confederate Army as a private on the day after the Virginia Convention had voted for secession and had risen to the rank of colonel. But all the ugliness he had seen over the past three years had not deprived him of civilized reaction, and he was about to show that all his courage had not been exhausted in cavalry charges.

He went to McCausland, as the general recounted the episode, and "asked me if it was being done by my orders. I showed him the order of General Early, which he refused to obey, declaring that he would break his sword and throw it away before he would obey it, as there were only defenseless women and children in Chambersburg." Upon hearing this, McCausland ordered Peters to collect his regiment and withdraw from the town, which he did. The general then had him put under arrest for insubordination.

There were other Confederates who, while not declaring outright their intent to disobey, helped civilians to escape. Some of the men obeyed only reluctantly. Most of the Confederates, however—hungry, weary, far from home, ill-equipped, badly armed, mounted on worn-out horses, and having drunk liberally from the contents of looted liquor stores—carried out their orders with abandon and, they believed, complete justification. "That it was right I never questioned, nor do I now," one participant wrote years later. "The responsibility rests on Gen'l Hunter."

A warehouse was the first to go, followed by the courthouse and town hall. General McCausland rode with an aide through the streets, pointing to the flames and smoke, notifying the residents that his threat had not been an idle one. The main part of the town was enveloped in flames within ten minutes.

The Confederates formed into squads and fanned out from the center of town. For two hours they rushed from house to house, burst open the doors with planks and axes, rifled every room for jewelry, silverware, and money, hacked up the

The stately columns from the portico of the Bank of Chambersburg survived the fires set by the Confederates. At left are the remains of a hotel known as the Franklin House.
HISTORICAL SOCIETY OF PENNSYLVANIA

furniture for kindling, and put torches to bedding and bureaus or lit balls of cotton saturated with kerosene. Some people were given time to collect a few belongings before their houses were fired; others were not. Describing the scene, a Confederate captain said: "It was impossible at first to convince the people, the females particularly that their fair city would [be] burnt; even when the torch was applied, they seemed dazed. Terror was depicted in every face, women, refined ladies and girls running through the streets wild with fright seeking some place of safety." Then he added soberly: "I hadn't bargained for this, but such it was."

One old woman was told by a Confederate squad to run, that her house was on fire. Her reply that she had not been able to walk for three years

was met with curses, and one of the soldiers poured powder under her chair, saying *he* would teach her to walk. Neighbors later rescued her.

A squad of Confederates demanded their breakfast of the local schoolmaster. "Did you ever teach niggers?" asked a cavalryman.

"Yes, sir," the schoolmaster replied.

"Damn him, fire his house," came the quick command.

The widow of a Union soldier begged for mercy. In response soldiers set fire to her house and robbed her of her money.

Not all the Confederates behaved so savagely. Reminded by a woman that she had fed him during a raid in 1862 and nursed him after the Battle of Gettysburg, one soldier shrank from firing the woman's house. A

CONTINUED ON PAGE 97

39

Among the legacies from the Depression of the 1930's, along with the fear and hunger of those crippling years, is an impressive national treasure of creative work—an artistic archive paid for by the government. Many projects that employed artists and writers were conceived specifically as a means of providing jobs. Some, however, including the photographic project of the Farm Security Administration, were essentially propagandistic. In financing the FSA pictures the government wanted to provide proof that its farm programs were needed and working. It was incidental to the government's purpose that the pictures formed a unique archive of those years.

Incidental, but not—as it turns out—accidental. Roy Stryker, who headed the photographic unit, "had a hunch" that the photographers working for him were producing pictures of more than temporary value. That he was right was unforgettably demonstrated in 1962 when the Museum of Modern Art in New York held a show about the Depression called "The Bitter Years," consisting entirely of FSA photographs. Stryker liked the show but was disappointed that the late Edward Steichen, who selected the material, had not chosen any of "the positive pictures."

Now, at eighty, Stryker has made his own selection—a group of pictures that he feels makes a powerful statement about America. Approximately two hundred of these photographs, with an accompanying text by Nancy Wood, will be published by the New York Graphic Society later this fall under the title In This Proud Land. In the following portfolio we present our selection of Mr. Stryker's selection—emphasizing some of the less well-known pictures from this remarkable collection—and an excerpt adapted from Nancy Wood's introductory portrait of Roy Stryker.

We pick up the Wood text when Stryker was called to Washington in 1935 by Rexford Guy Tugwell, the Undersecretary of Agriculture. Tugwell had been Stryker's teacher and mentor at Columbia University in New York, where Stryker had come to study and then teach economics. Knowing of Stryker's passion for documentary photography, Tugwell offered him an irresistible job.

"In This Proud Land"

By ROY STRYKER

and

NANCY WOOD

AMERICAN HERITAGE
BOOK SELECTION

This quiet, evocative still life by Walker Evans shows a general store in Moundville, Alabama, in 1936.

Text by NANCY WOOD

Considering how crucial Roy Stryker's shift from teaching to government service was to his whole future, Stryker describes the circumstances with amazing casualness.

"Tugwell went to Washington in the exciting early days of the New Deal," he says, "and shortly thereafter he sent for me to come down and work with him. In this way he gave me my great chance. He wanted to prepare a pictorial documentation of our rural areas and rural problems, something that had always been dear to my heart.

"But I didn't know how to go about doing the job he wanted me to—and he sensed it. One day he brought me into the office and said to me, 'Roy, a man may have holes in his shoes, and you may see the holes when you take the picture. But maybe your sense of the human being will teach you there's a lot more in that man than the holes in his shoes, and you ought to try and get that idea across.'"

That was in the summer of 1935. How was Stryker to picture what was behind the man with the holes in his shoes? He looked at his official job description. His duties were to ". . . direct the activities of investigators, photographers, economists, sociologists and statisticians engaged in the accumulation and compilation of reports . . . statistics, photographic material, vital statistics, agricultural surveys, maps and sketches necessary to make accurate descriptions of the various . . . phases of the Resettlement Administration [as the Farm Security Administration was originally called], particularly with regard to the historical, sociological and economic aspects of the several programs and their accomplishments."

It was just the sort of vague governmental mumble that Stryker detested. Probably few men at the time were more ill-suited to government work than he, and yet there he was, handed an unprecedented opportunity by Tugwell to do a particular job, but to do it as he pleased. He knew there *had* to be a picture file of rural problems, but what kind of picture file, and who would produce it?

Certainly not Stryker himself. Looking back at this time, he once remarked, "Perhaps my greatest asset was my lack of photographic knowledge. . . . I always had a camera, but I had no more business with that damn Leica than with a B-29. I got a hell of an inferiority complex because of it. My aunt and I once shot a family reunion. Her ten-dollar Brownie got everything, while I drew blanks. I never snapped a shutter after that. . . . My title in Washington was Chief of the Historical Section. My goal was to write the history of the Farm Security Administration. We didn't collect many documents. We collected pictures. Many think I went down to Washington with a big plan. I didn't. There was no such plan."

There may not have been a plan, but there was a clear mandate from Tugwell: get moving.

Slowly Stryker assembled his staff. The first to come was Arthur Rothstein, a chemistry major at Columbia who had taken a course in contemporary civilization under Stryker. At Columbia Rothstein had also copied thousands of pictures for him for a book about agriculture. He was dependable and a meticulous, skilled technician. He had just begun his photographic career by taking scientific pictures at a New York hospital. He would provide Stryker with the essentials of a darkroom.

Carl Mydans, with a strong background in journalism, was exploring everyday concerns with a camera in New York and trying unsuccessfully to sell his pictures to magazines. He was hired by Stryker, who was impressed with Mydans' warm and spontaneous approach to people.

At the same time arrived the most prestigious, particular, and temperamental photographer on the FSA team—Walker Evans. His pictures stood out from the lot with an unforgettable beauty. The only photographer to work with a large view camera, Evans took fewer pictures than anyone and spaced them over a longer period of time. Stryker eventually let him go because of his moodiness and his failure to produce the required number of photographs; the question of art was never involved. Today Evans' FSA pictures are regarded as the most artistic of all.

Soon after came Ben Shahn, a noted painter, lithographer, and muralist. Stryker recalls:

"Shahn came in from painting murals, and I put a Leica in his hands and said, 'Go out and fool around with it.' Shahn came back with pictures that were like his paintings—imaginative, beautiful things not restricted by technique. They were often out of focus and overexposed or underexposed. When Arthur or Walker Evans or Carl Mydans would get to worrying too much about technique, I'd bring out Shahn's photographs and say, 'Look at what Shahn has done and he doesn't know one part of a camera from another.'"

During that first fall, Stryker saw the pictures of Dorothea Lange, who had been deeply involved with the plight of California migrants. He was struck by her stark approach, and he felt that her pictures reflected a dignity of spirit that was unique. Later Stryker said that Lange "had the most sensitivity and the most rapport with people." She was quickly added to the payroll.

By the fall of 1935, with five of the most gifted photographers ever assembled, the FSA photo project was ready to start work.

The direction that the project took ignored governmental guidelines. Instead Stryker's convictions went to work. "I have nothing of the craftsman about me at all," he once explained to a colleague. "My only implement in life has been an insatiable curiosity about everything and every-

TEXT CONTINUES ON PAGE 55

Toilers on the Land

Before World War II one fourth of all Americans still lived on farms, and the FSA photographers recorded their work of producing the nation's food. Marion Post Wolcott caught the small figure below plowing with a hand-held plow a vast field in the Shenandoah Valley. Opposite, Russell Lee captured the careful movements of an elderly Texas farmer rolling barbed wire. In Vermont Jack Delano snapped a small boy bringing in the cows.

Small Coal and Big Steel

In the thirties there were still some individually owned coal mines, and Jack Delano photographed the coal-streaked miner opposite emerging with his pony from a mine near Penfield, Pennsylvania. Of the urban graveyard picture below, by Walker Evans, Roy Stryker recalled that after it was released, a woman came to his office and asked for a copy. "I want to give it to my brother who's a steel executive," she explained. "I want to write on it 'Your cemeteries, your streets, your buildings, your steel mills. But our souls, God damn you.'"

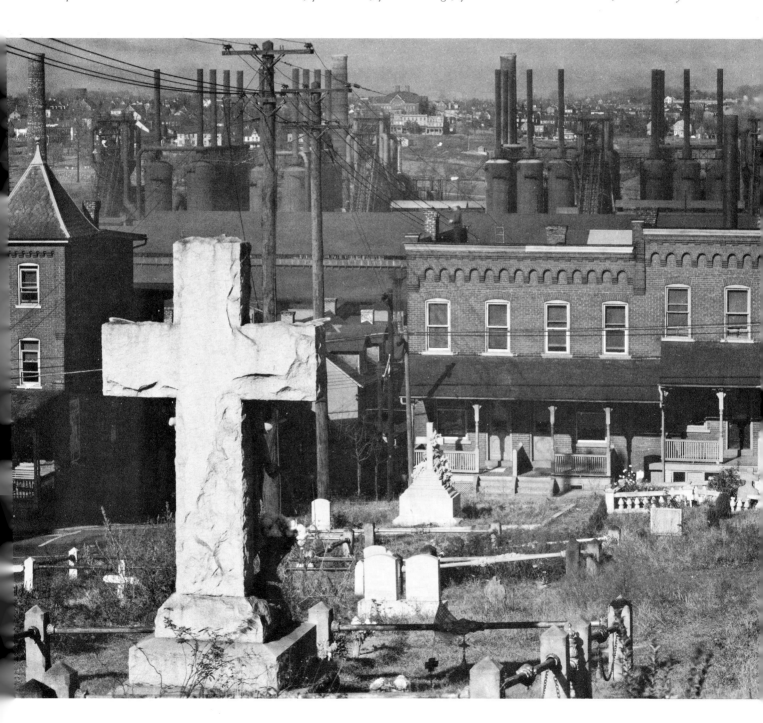

The Little Towns Were Dying

American small towns fascinated Roy Stryker, and the photographic unit, urged on by his probing questions ("How do various income levels dress when they go to church?"), assembled a pictorial archive of a passing way of life. "Through the pictures," Mr. Stryker said, "the small town emerged as a thing possessing emotional and esthetic advantages: kinship with nature and the seasons, neighborliness, kindliness, spaciousness—plus some certain disadvantages: laziness, pompousness, narrowness, lack of economic and cultural freedom." The two pictures here, taken in the mid-thirties, are of Mississippi towns. Opposite, Ben Shahn snapped two elderly ladies apparently dressed for church. And below, Dorothea Lange caught this highly symbolic tableau of a plantation owner and some of his employees.

47

In a cheerful mood, armed with scrub pails and twig brooms, the ladies of the congregation of Wheeley's Church in Person County,

North Carolina, pose for a picture before starting their annual thorough cleaning of the church. Dorothea Lange took the picture in 1939.

Faces
of the
Thirties

". . . the faces to me were the most significant part of the file," Stryker said in discussing the whole FSA picture collection. "Remember Steinbeck's famous lines— 'We ain't gonna die out. People is goin' on.' That's the feeling which comes through in those pictures. . . ." John Vachon photographed the travelling salesman in a hotel lobby in Elkins, West Virginia. The laughing couple were Polish tobacco farmers who lived near Windsor Locks, Connecticut, and Jack Delano took the picture. Opposite: Ben Shahn, the painter, turned loose with a camera, photographed this unforgettable mother and child in Arkansas.

The
Ill-housed
Third

Russell Lee, one of the later group of FSA photographers, took the two pictures on these pages of children in their shabby, pathetic homes. Stryker said of Lee's work: "When his photographs would come in, I always felt that Russell was saying, 'Now here is a fellow who is having a hard time but with a little help he's going to be all right.'" The small boy combing his hair below, his face distorted by the cracked mirror, was the son of a Missouri sharecropper. The little girls washing so carefully in their cramped bathtub lived in Oklahoma City.

body. I wanted to know why about everything. . . ."

Stryker translated his passion for "why" into specific guidelines for the photographers. This was when Stryker—the teacher, the economist, the man capable of communicating his enthusiasm to his staff—was at his best.

Before going out on assignment each member of the team was required to learn all he could about the area, its people, its economy, its political and social mores. The bible for the FSA photographers was J. Russell Smith's socioeconomic geography book, *North America*. In addition they carried maps, Department of Agriculture pamphlets, such magazines as *Harper's* and *Atlantic*, plus a "shooting script" prepared by Stryker that he has described as follows:

"Government was looser and more informal in those days than it is now. The bureaucratic web was such that my so-called official assignment memos—the photographers' shooting scripts—went like this: 'Bill posters; sign painters—crowd watching a window sign being painted; sky writing; paper in park after concert; parade watching, ticker tape, sitting on curb; roller skating; spooners-neckers; mowing the front lawn.' "

Both Stryker's ability to direct and his insistence that photographers go out armed with the facts are illustrated by a story he tells about one of Carl Mydans' first assignments:

"I remember one time when things were pretty bad down in the South and I assigned Carl to do a story about cotton. He had his bags packed and was going out the door, and I said to him, 'I assume you know something about cotton.' He said, 'No, not very much.' I called in my secretary and said, 'Cancel Carl's reservations. He's going to stay here with me for a while.' We sat down and we talked almost all day about cotton. We went to lunch and we went to dinner and we talked well into the night about cotton. I told him about cotton as an agricultural product, cotton as a commercial product, the history of cotton in the South, what cotton did to the history of the country, and how it affected areas outside the country. By the time we were through, Carl was ready to go off and photograph cotton."

As the photographs trickled back to Washington from the photographers, who sometimes went out for as long as six months at a time, Stryker knew what he was getting. He could hardly wait to open his mail in the mornings. He was excited, and so were the publications that were routinely given free use of the pictures and thereby brought to the attention of America what was happening to the one-third of a nation that was, in President Roosevelt's famous phrase, "ill-fed, ill-clad, and ill-housed." As a propaganda tool to help the New Dealers push through their farm programs, the FSA pictures proved a most vital asset. But they proved another thing, too: that America was not completely downtrodden, nor was it hopeless.

The government, however, often found it hard to accept the historical aspects of what Stryker was doing. Again and again he was criticized for not sticking to business, for wasting taxpayers' money, for bootlegging into a government file a lot of pictures of American life that had no use whatsoever—"silly sentimental pictures of women in bonnets." There was a congressional investigation. There were threats to cut off Stryker's funds. His staff was reduced. Time and again the photo unit seemed on the verge of oblivion. Time and again it was Tugwell who came to the rescue.

"The administration," Stryker admitted many years later, "simply could not afford to hammer home anything except their message that federal money was desperately needed for major relief programs. Most of what the photographers had to do to stay on the payroll was routine stuff showing what a good job the agencies were doing out in the field. . . . But we threw in a day here, a day there, to get what history has proved to be the guts of the project. . . . I'd tell the photographers, look for the significant detail. The kinds of things that a scholar a hundred years from now is going to wonder about. A butter churn. A horse trough. Crank-handle telephones. Front porches. The horse and buggy. The milk pails and the cream separators. Corner cupboards and wood stoves. Symbols of the time."

From 1937 until the end of the project in 1943 Stryker and the photographers working with him were constantly broadening their aims. By then new men were working in the photographic section: Russell Lee, Marion Post Wolcott, John Collier, Jr., John Vachon, Jack Delano, and, toward the end, Gordon Parks, the gifted black photographer. It was Stryker's goal to "record on film as much of America as we could in terms of people and the land. We photographed destitute migrants and average American townspeople, sharecroppers and prosperous farmers, eroded land and fertile land, human misery and human elation.

"What we ended up with was as well-rounded a picture of American life during that period as anyone could get. The pictures that were used were mostly pictures of the Dust Bowl and migrants and half-starved cattle. But probably half of the file contained positive pictures . . . country square dances and people listening to those big old radios, a soda jerk flipping a scoop of ice cream through the air, the mantel with the family portraits and the old Victorian clock, the nickel hamburger joints and the ten-cent barbershops . . . and then, of course, the big landscape

CONTINUED ON PAGE 81

Jack Delano photographed this tobacco worker, resting briefly on her hoe, near Durham, North Carolina, in 1940.

55

X MEN OF THE REVOLUTION

In war the final defeat is the one that counts. Yet there are wars and wars, and only rarely do historians conclude that a particular surrender was not only a cessation of fighting but a watershed marking the end of one epoch and the start of another. Otherwise there would be no memorable pairings of the vanquished with the scene of ultimate disaster—Harold and Hastings, Napoleon and Waterloo, Lee and Appomattox.

The curious thing about the defeat of Cornwallis at Yorktown is that the Americans in their moment of triumph saw it only as a great victory—not as *the* great victory. Even so, the final act was a superb piece of drama, for European armies of the day had a way of playing these scenes right, giving even defeat a touch of grandeur and pomp. Not surprisingly, Cornwallis refused to participate in the last rites; he claimed to be indisposed and remained at headquarters, sending a deputy to handle the unpleasant business. Then his British and German troops—many of them in new uniforms but with their flags cased—marched out between two half-mile-long lines of French and American soldiers and their ranks of waving banners, keeping step to the melancholy air of "The World Turn'd Upside Down" played by British bands and pipers. In their hour of humiliation some of the redcoats may have recalled the words to the old song:

> If ponies rode men and if grass ate the cows
> And cats should be chased into holes by the mouse . . .
> If summer were spring and the other way round,
> Then all the world would be upside down.

After watching Cornwallis' veterans file off to the surrender ground to lay down their arms, George Washington wrote a letter to Congress, describing the momentous occurrence only as an "Important Event" and voicing his concern that this success might produce "a relaxation in the prosecution of the war."

Not so in England, where six years of fighting had attuned men's ears to the relative significance of the outcome of battles. When news of Yorktown reached Lord North, George III's prime minister, he cried out, "Oh God! It is all over!" As indeed it was. Only the stubborn monarch desired to prolong the agony and revealed his intentions by drafting a notice of abdication rather than yield to the inevitable. Then he, too, perceived at last that the thing was done and turned despondently to leaders of the opposition to form a government, welcoming his new premier with the words "At last, the fatal day is come."

The wonder was that the man responsible for the defeat of British arms, the general remembered by generations of American schoolchildren only because he surrendered, got no blame for it from his countrymen. On the contrary, according to that august authority the *Encyclopaedia Britannica* (11th ed.), Cornwallis "not only escaped censure . . . but in 1786 received a vacant Garter, and was appointed governor-general of India and commander-in-chief in Bengal."

Charles, first Marquis and second Earl Cornwallis, was bred for better things than defeat at the hands of rebellious provincials. He not only possessed the requisites for success in the British army of the eighteenth century—position, money, and influence—he was also a man of uncommon intelligence and ability. The sixth child and eldest son of the first earl, he was born in 1738 and raised at Brome Hall near Eye, in Suffolk, which had been the family seat since the fourteenth century. He was educated at Eton, where he injured one eye in a hockey game, giving it a permanent cast (his biographers note that the accidental blow was struck by the Honorable Shute Barrington, later bishop of Durham). In 1756 he was commissioned an ensign in the Grenadier Guards, and from his eighteenth birthday on he took his career very seriously. He travelled on the Continent in the company of a tutor, who was a Prussian officer; studied at the military academy in Turin; campaigned during the Seven Years War in the army of Prince Ferdinand of Prussia; came home to England to be elected M.P. for the family borough; and when hostilities erupted in America, volunteered for service.

This was a surprise to George III, since Cornwallis had sided with the Whigs in opposition to his colonial policy; but the king genuinely liked and admired him. One of his strongest traits was loyalty—the sense of duty that prompted him to offer his services even though he knew he would not have the top command in America. Besides, he was a dignified, devoted family man, which counted for much with George, and in addition he was a considerable cut above the average military officer. He worked hard at being a successful commander, studied tactics, strategy, and administration, and paid more attention to his troops and their needs than most of his fellow officers ever thought of doing. Intelligent and compassionate, he did not hold with the cruel punishments that were commonplace in the army of his day; his men knew he was fair, they loved him for it, and would follow him unquestioningly. Sergeant Roger Lamb wrote of Cornwallis' own regiment, the 33rd, that he never saw any "that excelled it in discipline and military experience."

Cornwallis was thirty-eight when he arrived in America, a strong, imposing man with a full face, large nose, and heavy-lidded eyes, and during his first eighteen months of duty he proved that he was one of the best field commanders in the army. Serving under William Howe, he distinguished himself at Long Island, Kips Bay, White Plains, and Fort Washington; led the successful attack on Fort Lee; and harried Washington's army across New Jersey, restrained only by the dilatoriness of Howe. On January 2, 1777, he had Washington trapped at Trenton, but inexplicably permitted his intelligence to break down, as a result of which the rebels eluded him and attacked Princeton. After that momentary and costly lapse he added to his reputation at the battles of Brandywine and Germantown and then sailed for England to be with his ailing wife.

For all his ability, though, there was a flaw in Cornwallis' make-up somewhere that kept him from the ultimate success he dearly wanted. Maybe he loved his wife too well: Lady Jemima was an elegant, handsome, charming woman who was to die of a broken heart, it was said, caused by his protracted absence in

CHARLES EARL CORNWALLIS. 1783.

America. He missed her all the while he was away and maintained that her death in 1779 "effectually destroyed all my hopes of happiness in this world."

That was not the only problem, however. After he came back from England in 1779 to serve under Clinton, who had replaced Howe, bad blood broke out between the two at the siege of Charleston, and the feud continued for the rest of the war—Cornwallis alternately arrogant and sulky, Clinton peevish, petty, and suspicious. With Charleston in British hands Clinton returned to New York, leaving Cornwallis in command in the South, and in August of 1780 he overwhelmed Horatio Gates's army at Camden.

Disgusted with Clinton's passive strategy, he argued that instead of guarding British holdings in Georgia and South Carolina his southern army should take the offensive, move into North Carolina and Virginia, link up there with the northern army, and end the war. But in this he reckoned without Nathanael Greene, who became his opponent after Gates's defeat. Almost before Cornwallis realized it, Greene's hit-and-run tactics had forced him into a game of hare and hounds, stretching his supply lines near the breaking point, wearing out his men, driving him to the point where he complained of being "quite tired of marching about the Country in Quest of Adventure." Again and again Cornwallis demonstrated courage, fierce energy, resourcefulness, and initiative that nearly brought the war in the South to a close, but always he missed bringing the thing off, as if he became bored or distracted during periods of inaction and could not summon up the dedication necessary to finish the job.

One idea the earl never lost sight of was his plan to carry the offensive into Virginia, the most important of the states, and on April 10, 1781, he wrote to one of Clinton's deputies: "If we mean an offensive war in America, we must abandon New York, and bring our whole force into Virginia; we then have a stake to fight for, and a successful battle may give us America. If our plan is defensive, mixed with desultory expeditions, let us quit the Carolinas . . . and stick to our salt pork at New York, sending now and then a detachment to steal tobacco."

By June, American strength in the area was growing ominously, and Cornwallis fell back toward the coast; suddenly he decided to return to South Carolina and the scene of his earlier triumphs, only to receive word from Clinton ordering him to remain in Virginia and to hold Point Comfort until Admiral Thomas Graves arrived with the fleet. Instead Cornwallis chose to retire to the little village of Yorktown, where he began constructing fortifications as a protected anchorage for Graves. And there he was in September when the Comte de Grasse intercepted Graves and mauled his ships so badly that they were forced to return to New York for repairs. By then the combined armies of Washington and Rochambeau had ringed Cornwallis in, and the dénouement was at hand. On October 17, 1781, Lord Cornwallis sent a flag across the lines requesting a twenty-four-hour cessation of hostilities, and two days later his six thousand men marched out to lay down their arms.

Released on parole, he went first to New York, where the old quarrel with Clinton broke out again as each sought to absolve himself of the blame for Yorktown, and in January of 1782 Cornwallis sailed for England, where he was greeted more as a hero than a defeated general. Clinton was to be the goat; Cornwallis, it was argued, was merely a victim of circumstance.

Two years later, when Warren Hastings resigned as governor general of India, the young Prime Minister William Pitt decided that Cornwallis was the man to succeed Hastings, restore military and civil services in India, and at the same time repair Britain's prestige after the defeats in the recent Mysore war. Twice Cornwallis refused but finally accepted "much against his will and with grief of heart." He was no longer so intent on the will-o'-the-wisp of fame, it appeared. Yorktown had been a chastening experience, and he was even self-conscious about his election as a knight of the Garter. As he wrote his son after leaving for India, "You will very likely laugh at me for wishing to wear a blue riband over my fat belly. . . . But I can assure you upon my honour that I neither asked for it nor wished for it."

Out in India he set to work with characteristic vigor, instituting drastic civil and military reforms in Bengal; and when Tippoo Sahib of Mysore attacked a British ally in 1790, Cornwallis personally took command of the army, conducted a careful, well-conceived campaign, and two years later defeated Tippoo, finally breaking the power and prestige of the Mysore dynasty for good. (In addition to ceding half of his territories, Tippoo was forced to pay indemnities amounting to £3,600,000, and a grateful government awarded over £47,000 of it to Cornwallis, who promptly donated the entire amount to his troops.)

His job done, he returned to England in 1794 to be made master general of ordnance with a seat in Pitt's cabinet, and he was entrusted with the defenses of the country against an anticipated invasion by Bonaparte that failed to materialize. In 1798 Pitt turned to him again to perform a thankless task: the government badly needed a soldier-statesman to restore peace in Ireland, and Cornwallis was made viceroy and commander in chief of the British forces there. His immediate task was to suppress the rebellion, which he executed with dispatch; next he put the Act of Union into effect and in the meantime, having perceived that the Irish parliament did not represent the people of the country, urged its abolition and championed the right of Irish Catholics to sit in Parliament. But George III refused to hear of this, and in 1801 Cornwallis resigned. Back in England he learned that he had been appointed British plenipotentiary to negotiate a peace with Napoleon. Unhappily Cornwallis was neither a diplomatist nor a match for the combined wits of Joseph Bonaparte and Talleyrand, and the Treaty of Amiens, signed in 1802, proved to be a truce, not a peace.

For three years Cornwallis was permitted to rest; then came another urgent summons from the government, requesting him to return once again to India as governor general and commander in chief. Now sixty-six, he regarded the undertaking as foolhardy for a man his age; but the old sense of duty won out, and off he sailed in March of 1805, arriving to find a "most unprofitable and ruinous warfare" in India, which he moved at once to stop. Heading up the Ganges toward the scene of the fighting, he lost consciousness, and on October 5, 1805, he died.

Whether he had ever felt obliged to compensate for what occurred at Yorktown more than two decades earlier no one can say, but by his own lights a career was not measured in victories or defeats. "The reasonable object of ambition to man," he once wrote his son, "is to have his name transmitted to posterity for eminent services rendered to his country and mankind."

—*Richard M. Ketchum*

"1795.—The state of my health rendering a voyage to Europe necessary, I determined to proceed by way of America. Accordingly, towards the end of November, I left Santipore, taking with me a small Bengal cow, in addition to my doombah and other curiosities brought from Delhi. The natives would not have consented to sell me a cow if I had not assured them that it would be an object of particular interest and care in the countries I was taking it to."

The author was Thomas Twining, nineteen, son of a prosperous family of tea and coffee merchants who in 1706 had opened a shop in Devereux Court in the Strand, near Temple Bar, in London (the family is still in business today with the same products and the same name at the same address). Twining did indeed come to America with his Bengal cow, his doombah (an Afghan mountain sheep), and an extraordinary collection of other animals and artifacts.

Twining, a graduate of Rugby, had gone to India at sixteen as a "writer"—that is, a clerk—in the Honorable East India Company's Bengal Service, carrying with him a violin, a Persian grammar, and Dr. Johnson's dictionary. On his arrival in Calcutta he was placed in the financial department and was soon promoted to the posts of head assistant, acting subaccountant-general, and commissioner of the Court of Requests. Lord Cornwallis, the governor general, became his friend and patron, and when Twining's health, never strong, began to fail, Cornwallis moved him to higher, healthier, mosquito-free land by making Twining assistant to the Resident of Santipur. It was a position, Cornwallis said, that he would have given his own son under similar circumstances. Apparently it was also a post with some risks, however, for once, in order to escape bandits, Twining pulled down the curtains of his palanquin and instructed his bearers to say that he was a lady of the imperial se-

Protégé of Cornwallis, Guest of Washington

Thomas Twining

By ROBERT C. ALBERTS

raglio, whom they wouldn't dare rob.

The Great Mogul, emperor of the 250-year-old Moslem empire in India, graciously consented to receive Twining on his throne in Delhi and permitted him to commemorate the event with a silver tablet engraved in Persian characters. Twining resolved to match this distinction with another. He would travel to America and there be received by President George Washington, ruler of the New World.

He booked passage for himself and his servant on the *India,* a three-hundred-ton, three-masted vessel 357 days out of Philadelphia on her second voyage to the Far East. She was owned by William Bingham and Mordecai Lewis of Philadelphia and their partner, Robert Gilmore of Baltimore. Her captain was John Ashmead, a tall, slim, upright man whose "thin silvery locks curled round the collar of his old-fashioned single-breasted coat."

In the spirit of scientific inquiry, Twining had collected for the voyage a rich variety of examples of Indian life and culture. An ingenious workman in Santipur had made him small but exact models of the principal machines and instruments used in agriculture and industry. He bought at auction a number of oil paintings of Indian scenes done by a European artist. He acquired the bottom half of an oyster shell weighing more than a hundred pounds. To his doombah and cow he added a great Kabul sheep, a monkey from the north of India, and a specimen of the Tibetan goat, the source of cashmere, commonly but erroneously thought to derive from a species of sheep. For his comfort he bought a teakwood bedstead with built-in drawers and a hanging apparatus that could convert the bed into a swinging cot in rough weather. Since American captains had "the reputation of keeping rather an indifferent table—living, it was said, principally on salt beef and sour-crout," Twining sent aboard

Travels in India 100 Years Ago, REV. W. H. G. TWINING, ED. (JAMES R. OSGOOD, MCILVAINE & CO., LONDON, 1893); COURTESY THE READING ROOM, BRITISH MUSEUM

ten fat sheep and "a considerable quantity of hay."

The *India* sailed down the Ganges with her cargo of cloth and spices, set a course for the Cape of Good Hope, and began what was to be a voyage of almost four months and almost fourteen thousand miles. Twining read, exercised, played backgammon with Captain Ashmead, and talked with the surgeon, the chief mate, the supercargo, Mr. Pringle, and Mr. Gilmore, the son of one of the owners, who was learning the business of an eastern voyage. The crew, he found, was made up of twenty-two very young men, "sons of respectable families of Philadelphia and Baltimore, who had come to sea . . . preparatory to their being officers and captains themselves." From time to time the *India* hailed passing ships in the open sea and stopped to throw a line for exchanging newspapers, letters, and longitudinal readings. Twining remarked that throughout the voyage he never heard the captain make a threat or any sailor utter an oath.

Off the coast of North America on April 2 the leadsman proclaimed bottom, and three days later the *India* took on a pilot and entered Delaware Bay.

Having passed several ships, the *India* entered the line, and took her station along one of the wharfs, which extended nearly the whole length of the city, and in a few minutes I *stepped ashore* without even the aid of a plank, the ship's side touching the wharf.

It being evening, when many people were about, the quay was crowded with persons curious to witness an arrival from Bengal.

He made a few turns up and down the wharf, managed to get a porter, and started off with his trunk for the London Tavern. Mr. Pringle, the supercargo, came up and urged him to pay a call first on Mordecai Lewis.

This worthy citizen received me very kindly, saying "How dost thou do, friend? I am glad to see thee"; for he was, in the phraseology of Philadelphia,

one of the Society of Friends, that is to say, a Quaker. He introduced me to Mrs. Lewis and his daughters, who received me with the same salutation, "I am glad to see thee, friend; I hope thou art well." I drank tea with these good people, in whom I found a kindness which the simplicity of their manners seemed to make the more cordial. The safe arrival of their ship at a favorable market put all the family in good spirits.

After tea Pringle took him to call on Lewis' partner, William Bingham.

Mr. Bingham . . . was the principal person in Philadelphia and the wealthiest, probably, in the Union. His house [at Third and Spruce streets] stood alone and occupied, with the gardens attached to it, a spacious piece of ground. It was by far the handsomest residence in the city. I found here a large party. . . . Mr. Bingham, the President of the Pennsylvania State, not only gave me a general invitation to his house, but offered to take care of my great sheep during my stay in America.

Twining dined at the Binghams' and returned to spend the night at Lewis' house. His sleep and sense of propriety were disturbed after an hour when a stranger crawled into bed with him.

I inferred . . . that in America, when a stranger was invited to pass the night with his host, it was never meant to give him the whole of a bed. When the light of the morning shown upon the features of my companion, whose face should I see but Mr. Pringle's. . . . I felt that I could not reasonably complain, for as his attentions had procured me this bed, no one certainly had so fair a claim to half of it as himself.

Twining took a room the next morning at the London Tavern, but finding it "deficient in comfort," he sallied forth in search of better quarters. Where, he asked a passer-by, did the members of Congress stay? Many of them, he was told, lived together in a house on Fourth Street kept by an old Frenchman named Francis. Mr. Francis rudely declined

to take him in, but on learning that he was newly arrived from India "repeated, in a tone of diminished repugnance almost amounting to civil regret, that his house was full." Mrs. Francis, his young American wife, intervened to offer Twining a small room at the top of the house, which he might change in a day or two for one next to that occupied by John Adams, the Vice President. The maidservant who showed him upstairs was a Negro woman, the property of Mr. Francis, "young, active, obliging, and spoke English." It was Twining's first encounter with slavery in America, and he was disturbed: "It caused me both pain and surprise to meet with it in the country which so boasted of the freedom of its institutions."

At dinner that noon and at tea, both presided over by Mrs. Francis, he met several members of the two houses of Congress "and thought them most amiable, sensible men." Twining congratulated himself on his good fortune at "being already established in the most respectable society of the United States." He breakfasted the next morning "at the public table," again with several congressmen and senators.

Mrs. Francis helped me to some of the celebrated buckwheat cake, whose excellence had been the subject of much commendation during our voyage. . . . It is superior to the crumpet or muffin, having the peculiar taste of the buckwheat, which is extremely agreeable. . . .

After breakfast he called on Bingham, to inspect his animals.

. . . I found my doombah grazing upon the garden lawn at the back of the house. While I was looking at it with Mr. Bingham, several inhabitants of the city came to gratify their curiosity, for Mr. Bingham, having observed this, had ordered that everybody should be admitted, and considerable numbers had already come to the garden in consequence. My Bengal cow, which I found in a stable not far off, also had numerous visitors.

Twining that day presented his oyster shell to Charles Willson Peale, the artist and naturalist, for his National Museum ("it was very graciously accepted") and called on Mr. Bond, the British consul. "He asked me many questions about India and said he must introduce me to General Washington."

I dined with the Members of Congress. Mr. Adams took the chair always reserved for him at the head of the table, though himself superior to all sense of superiority. He appeared to be about sixty years of age. In person he was rather short and thick; in his manner somewhat cold and reserved, as the citizens of Massachusetts, his native state, are said generally to be. His presence caused a general feeling of respect, but the modesty of his demeanour and the tolerance of his opinions excluded all inconvenient restraint. He was generally dressed in a light or drab-coloured coat, and had the appearance rather of an English country gentleman who had seen little of the world, than of a statesman who had seen so much of public life.

The next day Dr. Ross, an English physician, called to take him to visit Dr. Joseph Priestley, "a celebrated man of whom I had heard a great deal when a boy at school." A scientist and nonconformist minister, Fellow of the Royal Society and frequent lecturer at the American Philosophical Society, renowned for his discoveries in electricity and chemistry, Priestley had expressed such unorthodox political and religious views, and such sympathy for the French revolutionists, that an infuriated Birmingham mob broke into his house, pillaged his library, burned his notes and manuscripts, and destroyed his "philosophical apparatus." He received compensation for the damage, but in 1794 he emigrated to the United States.

Dr. Ross, in his friendly zeal, introduced me [to Priestley] somewhat in the style of a showman at a country fair: "Mr. Twining—just arrived from Bengal—a great traveller on the Ganges—has been received by the Great Mogol," etc. The Doctor, his simplicity unchanged by this recital, received me with hearty kindness. He placed me near the fire and took a chair by my side. I soon found that he was as inquisitive as Dr. Ross had represented him to be. Fortunately his inquiries were directed to such subjects respecting India as were familiar to me, such as the castes, customs, and character of the inhabitants; climate, productions, etc.

The Doctor related, in his turn, many anecdotes. . . . He had a way, when telling his stories, of asking you to *guess* how a thing happened, saying, "Now, sir, how do you think this was?" waiting a few moments for an answer. Among other things, he spoke of the great sheep in Mr. Bingham's garden, expressing his intention of seeing it, and then alluded to the great improvement lately made by Mr. Bakewell of Leicestershire in the breed and management of animals. He said he once visited Mr. Bakewell, who showed him . . . his fine bulls, remarkable for their size and symmetry. He saw two of these animals grazing peaceably in the same pasture. "I can," said Mr. Bakewell, "immediately make these bulls as furious as they are now quiet, and again make them friends." "And how," said the Doctor, addressing himself to me, ". . . do you think this was done? Why, sir, Mr. Bakewell ordered one of his men to drive a cow into the field, and the two bulls rushed at each other, and fought with great fierceness. Whilst they were thus engaged, the cow was driven out of the field, and the two champions grazed together quietly as before."

The Tibetan goat had died shortly before the arrival in Philadelphia, but Twining had saved the skin, and Priestley expressed a desire to examine it. Accordingly, he appeared next day with his son Joseph and went with Twining to the *India,* which was still discharging its cargo. He studied the skin with much care, turning back the long hair and feeling the downy wool beneath, and finally allowed that cashmere was indeed the produce of a goat. "I thought I could not dispose of this curiosity better than by placing it in his possession," Twining wrote, "and requested the Doctor to allow one of the sailors to carry it to his house. Although he yielded to this proposal with reluctance, I had the satisfaction of perceiving that it afforded him pleasure."

Upon separating from Dr. Ross, I went to the house where the Congress held its meetings, situated in Chestnut Street. It is a large and handsome building, occupying the area of an extensive court, by the side of the street. . . .

. . . Mr. Gallatin was speaking. Mr. Gallatin is a native of France or Switzerland, but had long resided in America. . . .

Twining had occasion to meet with Gallatin when the latter appeared at breakfast at the Francis house on April 13 along with members of Congress, "with whom," Twining wrote, "I was now upon easy terms." Gallatin examined Twining's muslin neckcloth and was surprised at what it had cost in India. That touched off a spirited discussion about both the quality and the prices of Indian fabrics, but mostly about the prices, which Twining noted "suggested the idea of a profitable speculation, the object of almost every American at this period."

Three days later Twining began a "rough and fatiguing" four-week journey to Baltimore and on to Washington, the new Federal City then under construction. He rode in a long ten-passenger "waggon" with a light roof and side curtains made of leather that might be raised or lowered, but without backs to the unpadded wood benches. Despite the wretched roads and the intolerable jolting of the springless wagon, Twining observed approvingly that "everywhere the progress of improvement was visible; everything had advanced and was advancing. . . . It would be unreasonable to expect perfection in the arrangements of a new country. . . . I believe there is no nation that would have done more in so short a time, and most nations would assuredly have done infinitely less." And:

CONTINUED ON PAGE 98

While Jumbo looks on weeping, at top, the British Lion demands his release from P. T. Barnum's circus and his return to England. (Our headline reproduces that of an original Barnum flyer.) The exuberant poster depicts Jumbo's size with only normal exaggeration.

TOP: *Harper's Weekly*, JUNE 3, 1882; BOTTOM: AMERICAN ANTIQUARIAN SOCIETY

It is a warm summer evening in 1882, in a small town in New England, and the circus of Messrs. Barnum, Bailey, and Hutchinson has come to town for a one-day stand. The "Greatest Show on Earth" is suitably canopied: three huge tents in a meadow on the outskirts of town—one tent each for the museum and the freak collections, and the big one, the one with four rings that seats thirty thousand people, towers in the middle. In this

the size claimed by the showman Barnum; but as the drum roll reaches a crescendo and the giant African bull elephant begins slowly to pace the circle of the hippodrome, they sit up and gasp. Words fail them—he is unbelievable, yet there he is, striding before them with untold power and magnificent grace, literally dwarfing every living creature within the range of visual comparison.

Jumbo's capsule biography would

vier, current assistant director, says that both elephants were received on October 20, 1863, not from Schmidt but from the viceroy of Egypt.

About a year and a half later the Jardin des Plantes found itself overstocked with elephants but wanted to acquire a rhinoceros, while at the same time the London Zoo was trying to locate another elephant to join its herd of five and happened to have an extra rhino on hand. When Lon-

Pried loose from a furious Great Britain to meet a

tragic death in the New World, this huge elephant made a fortune for his owner,

delighted millions, and added a new superlative to our language

big top the smell of sawdust hangs thick in the air, and although as the evening wears on some of the ladies begin to wish the brass band would not play quite so loudly, their men and children lighten the sweltering heat with cheers—cheers for the lion tamers and trapeze artists and clowns in the middle three rings and for the stunning bareback riders in the outer ring, the Roman hippodrome.

The displays continue unabated until, suddenly, there is a hush as the splendidly dressed ringmaster, with the accompaniment of a heavy drum roll, begins his introduction, drawling in the unmistakable circus accent the traditional "LADEEZ AND GENTLE-MEN!" The people know what he is announcing. They have read the papers, and they know that Phineas Taylor Barnum has recently acquired from the British, by hook and crook, the hugest animal on the face of the earth, the largest elephant seen by modern man, the mighty Jumbo. They have seen the posters that bill him as a "Feature Crushing All Attempts At Fraud / The Towering Monarch of His Mighty Race / Whose Like the World will never See Again."

That's a tall order to fill, and they wonder if any beast could truly reach

read that he was the largest elephant ever kept in captivity, a record undisputed to the present day; no animal in history has had so much written about him (with such a large portion of it pure nonsense) as P. T. Barnum's celebrated Jumbo. Yet when people today are asked what they know about Jumbo, perhaps half of them recall that he was a circus elephant from past days who was called Jumbo because he was so big. This is an error at the outset. It was the giant animal whose name was given to outsized objects, not the other way around. He himself was christened Jumbo when he was less than five feet tall.

Of the many "authorities" who have written on Jumbo, nearly every one contradicts some others on points of his life, character, and death. One of the few things that all sources agree upon is that Jumbo was captured as a baby in Africa, most probably by Hamran Arabs somewhere in Ethiopia. The infant beast spent some time in Cairo, where he was taken, along with another baby elephant, by the Bavarian animal collector Johann Schmidt. Although most writers maintain that Schmidt sold the animals directly to the Jardin des Plantes, or Paris zoo, Dr. Guy Chau-

don suggested a swap, Paris was "delighted" and even threw in two spiny anteaters.

On his arrival in London the "elephantine toddler," as one newspaper referred to him, was the first African elephant to be shown in England, and he was given the name Jumbo, a shortened form of Mumbo Jumbo, after a kind of priest who allegedly protects west African villages from evil spirits. Jumbo, as it turned out, needed protection himself; when his crate was opened, he was found to be half starved, severely ill, and near death. Assigned as one of Jumbo's caretakers was Matthew Scott, an underkeeper who, with some others, spent months nursing the infant to glowing health. Thereafter Jumbo and "Scotty" became inseparable.

As the years passed, Jumbo grew steadily, both in height and in the esteem of the British people. He was totally devoted to his keeper and was so gentle he became the favorite riding animal in the zoo. As he grew to eleven feet in height, the managers of the London Zoo realized that their young charge had become the largest animal in captivity in the world. Jumbo was something of an institution, a national pet, said *Harper's Weekly,* and "as gentle with children as the best-

By JAMES L. HALEY

JUMBO REFUSING TO LEAVE THE ZOO.

JUMBO'S REFUSAL TO ENTER THE BOX.

trained poodle dog, taking the proffered biscuit or lump of sugar with an almost incredible delicacy of touch. . . . The most nervous child, having once overcome his alarm, never hesitated to hand a morsel to his waving trunk a second time." Any day of the week he could be seen quietly plodding the gravel paths of the zoo in Regent's Park, the topless howdah strapped to the broad back filled with six or eight goggle-eyed children. By the early 1880's the total number carried was in the hundreds of thousands.

Among Jumbo's admirers was the greatest showman of all time, Phineas Taylor Barnum. To put it summarily, he came, he saw, he coveted. If Barnum had Jumbo in his circus, it would mean millions of dollars to the show. With apparently hopeless bravado Barnum instructed his man in London to approach the directors of the Royal Zoological Society and explore the possibility that they might part with their mountainous attraction. He did not know, of course, how astonishingly lucky he was. The London Zoo had been trying for months to get rid of Jumbo.

There were two reasons. The directors were fearful that Jumbo, near adulthood, would soon fall victim to musth, the periodic inflammation of the male elephant's temporal glands (it was not known at this time that musth is apparently limited to the Asiatic species). While the con-

dition lasts it can drive the elephant berserk, and the gigantic Jumbo, in such a state, could do irreparable damage.

The second problem was his devotion to Scott. Jumbo's affection for the man was such that he could not bear to be separated from him for a moment. At night, when Scott was not there, Jumbo would throw tantrums that nearly wrecked the elephant house. If Scott were to die suddenly, the elephant's grief would be murderous.

Such was the situation when Barnum's London agent approached Mr. P. L. Sclater, the secretary of the R.Z.S., to inquire whether or not the zoo could be induced to part with its star attraction; and although the society behaved with tasteful reluctance, its officers privately thought the offer a godsend and did not reject the idea as expected. When this news was cabled to Barnum, the old showman, then seventy-two, rifled back an offer of ten thousand dollars, the equivalent of two thousand pounds sterling. London delayed for just two days, and then it was done. The deal was closed, and Jumbo was sold.

In accordance with strict zoo policy the transaction was still a secret. But Barnum wasn't satisfied; bombast was his trademark, and as soon as it was safe to do so (that is, as soon as the sealed and irrevocable contract was delivered safe into the hands of his own men), he ordered his press

army to go to work and make the British people feel that they had been swindled. His reason was clarified by one writer in 1933: "In order to make the American Public realize what it was gaining, Mr. Barnum had to make the British Public realize what it was losing." And Mr. Barnum, as usual, pulled the strings perfectly. When he let the news break, the story "burst like a bomb" on England, and the reaction was a national temper tantrum, which delighted the showman. Editors lamented; John Ruskin wrote with firm Britannic iciness that England had not been in the habit of selling her pets; the Prince of Wales, the colorful Albert Edward, publicly condemned the transaction. It was rumored that Queen Victoria herself believed privately that the Zoological Society should refuse to deliver the goods and let the state assume responsibility. And this furor was only the beginning.

The morning after Barnum received the cable indicating the zoo's acceptance of his offer, he dispatched his head elephant keeper, William Newman, to arrange and oversee Jumbo's journey to the United States. Stepping off the ship in Lon-

Bringing Jumbo to America was a tough job, as these pictures from a circus flyer suggest. Barnum spent thirty thousand dollars on the elephant, but Jumbo earned it back during his first two weeks in the States.
ALL: CANADIAN NATIONAL RAILWAYS

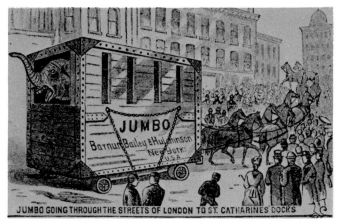

JUMBO GOING THROUGH THE STREETS OF LONDON TO ST. CATHARINES' DOCKS

JUMBO BEING LOADED ON THE STEAMER "ASSYRIAN MONARCH."

don, "Elephant Bill," as he was called, expected no trouble at all in getting Jumbo from the zoo through six miles of streets to St. Katherine's Docks on the Thames, in a travelling cage that he would have constructed. There the elephant would be hoisted aboard the steamship *Persian Monarch*. In fact, however, the departure was delayed for nearly two months, during which Barnum happily reaped further publicity. He was aided in the slowdown by the stubbornness and cupidity of Matthew Scott.

The travelling cage was nearly a month in the building, but finally, pulled on a huge four-wheeled trolley by a half-dozen magnificent dray horses, it called for Jumbo at the zoo on Saturday, February 11, 1882. Scott managed to coax his elephant as far as the wooden ramp leading to the cage, and then he retired inconspicuously to the door of the elephant house. Jumbo, at the urging now of

Newman and A. D. Bartlett, director of the zoo, placed a ponderous forefoot on the planks but could be induced to go no farther. When two hours of gentle persuasion and sugared buns did not convince him, they had to give in and call Scott to come lead Jumbo back to the elephant house for the night.

Nothing daunted, Newman conceived a new plan. Tomorrow he would walk Jumbo to the river, where, in quieter surroundings, he would be less apt to balk. The British press, it seems, had decided that Jumbo hesitated only because of a true sense of loyalty to English soil, but it was his behavior the next day that made English hearts go out more than ever to their beleaguered pet.

Bright and early on February 12 Jumbo plodded with his characteristic grace behind Scott down the gravel paths of the zoo to the entrance gate, thence to be led on foot to the

dock from which he would embark.

Halfway through the gate the animal stopped short and then backed nervously into the zoo grounds again. Scott, in earshot of a horde of reporters, began to scold the elephant coarsely. Jumbo caressed Scott piteously with his trunk and moaned and whimpered so loudly that the birds in the nearby parrot house screeched in terror, starting up a wave of frightened tumult that reached to the far ends of the zoo. Then Scott, to all outward appearances trying to calm the elephant, put his finger to his lips, and abruptly Jumbo groaned louder than ever and rolled over onto his side, seven tons of "immovable obstinacy." No one present knew that Jumbo was trained to lie down at that particular signal. Scott was staging the entire business.

Reporters, believing (wrongly) that the loudest din was being raised by a cow elephant, Alice, whom

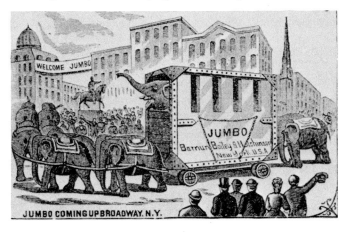

JUMBO COMING UP BROADWAY. N.Y.

THE PALACE CAR IN WHICH JUMBO TRAVELS.

Big as he was, Jumbo was too small to match Barnum's vaunting ambitions. To the right an illustration from a handbill depicts him as a house-sized behemoth undisturbed by the carriage passing underneath. The photograph shows the real Jumbo—puny by comparison, but still a lot of elephant—with his keeper, Matthew Scott.

they believed (also wrongly) to be Jumbo's mate, sensed the news break of the year. They dashed off in hansom cabs to file their stories while Scott led Jumbo back to the elephant house and Newman presumably threw up his hands. Whether the American saw through Scott or was purposely playing fall guy remains a fascinating question. But the fact is that he changed Jumbo's reservation to the *Assyrian Monarch,* which would not sail until the twenty-fifth of March, and cabled to his boss in New York: "Jumbo is lying in the garden and will not stir. What shall we do?" And Barnum, with characteristic sauce, replied: "Let him lie there as long as he wants to. The publicity is worth it."

In the ensuing weeks publicity was plentiful. British hucksters were not ignorant of the storm of mawkish sympathy, and they immediately cranked out an avalanche of Jumbo products. There were Jumbo boots, Jumbo perfumes, Jumbo earrings, and Jumbo cigars, not to mention Jumbo letterheads, ties, fans, hats, collars, overcoats, and underwear. Much poetry was written on the subject—little of it good, though one versifier suggested a remarkable remedy:

> *But since in England's fallen state*
> *She owns two things supremely great,*
> *Jumbo and Gladstone—(each we find*
> *The most prodigious of their kind)—*
> *And one won't budge. Then, Barnum, make*
> *A fair exchange for quiet's sake!*
> *Take the Right Honourable and go!*
> *He'll make the better raree show!*
> *Leave Jumbo.*

Fund drives were started by the more hopeful zealots in an attempt to ransom their Jumbo from the clutches of Barnum and save him for Britain's children. Barnum's florid answers to their sponsors' offers gave him further opportunity to advertise his circus. And as the public temper over Jumbo rose daily, so did the number of his visitors. On one day in March, 1882, Jumbo was seen by 4,626 sorrowing admirers (compared with a crowd of 214 the same day a year before), many of whom brought gifts to the elephant, which naturally were presented to his keeper. Therein lay one reason why Scott was delaying the removal for as long as possible. He was getting rich! So was the zoo. Packed farewell receptions for Jumbo, on the grounds, grossed fifty thousand dollars to its treasury. It was suggested in the London *Fun* that the British lion be removed from the coat of arms and be replaced by the celebrated elephant, with the motto *Dieu et Mon Jumbo.*

At last, after all appeals to Barnum's sense of moral decency and indignant letters to the *Times* fell on

deaf ears, Britons went to the courts. Some Fellows of the Royal Zoological Society brought an action in chancery for an injunction against Jumbo's removal. The suit raised intriguing questions about the powers and purposes of the society under its charter, but in the end it failed in the Court of Queen's Bench before Mr. Justice Chitty, who ruled that public remorse over a perfectly legal transaction was not enough to cancel the contract.

By early March, Barnum had gained free publicity worth considerably more than the ten-thousand-dollar price tag. Meanwhile, the real reason for Jumbo's stubbornness was beginning to dawn on Director Bartlett of the zoo. He had realized that Jumbo went wherever Scott led him but, fearful of becoming separated from his beloved keeper, refused to be sent away; and that Scott had carefully refrained from leading Jumbo toward the travelling cage or the dock. Now, having an ace to play and sick both of the whole Jumbo mess and of being blackmailed by Scott, Bartlett first sought out Newman and

66

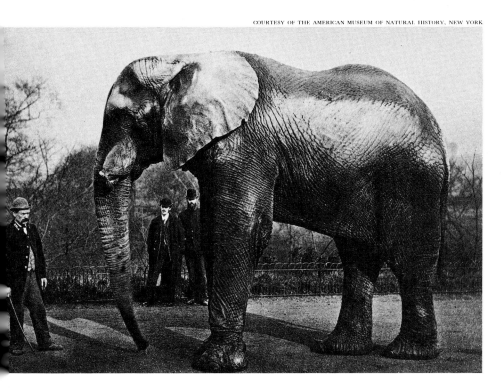

"convinced" him of what was untrue —that Scott's presence was a hindrance and that at the next loading attempt he would have better luck if Scott were absent. Then Bartlett laid down the law to his troublesome underkeeper: Jumbo would be leaving England with or without him. Scott chose to go along.

On Wednesday, March 15, Newman had the cage placed in position once more, and Scott led Jumbo to the door, where the huge elephant paused a moment, testing the floor, then lumbered calmly inside. He was hauled to St. Katherine's Docks, put on a lighter, and floated two miles downstream to the *Assyrian Monarch*. It took but eight minutes to hoist cage and elephant aboard and lower them into their specially reinforced hold. Throughout most of the trip Scott was perched on the front of the cage, holding Jumbo's trunk, and the great animal showed no fright at all.

Jumbo took the crossing well and consumed in transit some two tons of hay, two sacks of biscuits and three of oats, and one sack of his favorite treat, onions.

The *Assyrian Monarch*, with its unlikely cargo, arrived in New York on April 9, and the next morning a puffing P. T. Barnum clambered over the rail, closely followed by his entourage of reporters, to whom he exclaimed: "Dear old Jumbo. That beast has cost me fifty thousand dollars." Though Barnum inflated the transportation costs for the press, he cannily labelled Jumbo as "breeding stock" and thus escaped paying any import duties on him.

Scott had been hired by Barnum to continue as Jumbo's keeper, since he was indispensable to control the animal. And Scott, difficult as ever, demanded his own terms—and got them. When somebody produced a quart of whiskey, the keeper without hesitation gave it to Jumbo. Barnum, a believer in temperance, was aghast. "I object to my elephant's drinking whiskey!" he sputtered. But Scott paid no more attention to Barnum than he had paid to Bartlett. He gave Jumbo a chaser of ale and affirmed that the elephant got beer daily and, when feeling poorly, a medicinal dose of two gallons of whiskey.

Sober or not, Jumbo had arrived in New York in time for the annual circus opening at Madison Square Garden, and he was transported through streets packed with cheering throngs while posters and advertisements crowed "TOM THUMB and JENNY LIND . . . retire into Obscurity when viewed in the Full Blaze of the DAZZLING JUMBO." Other circulars boasted of how Barnum had singlehandedly defeated the British government, people, and court system. Jumbo was a financial venture—a thirty-thousand-dollar venture— and Barnum was making every effort to get his money back. And Jumbo at the Garden proved once again that Barnum's instincts were never wrong; the mighty elephant chalked up receipts of more than three thousand dollars a day, so that by the end of two weeks Jumbo had returned his new owner the entire thirty thousand dollars, as well as a clear net profit of 20 per cent.

When the Greatest Show on Earth went out on its annual tour, Jumbo proved to be just as popular on the road as he was in New York, shattering all previous records of income; and if he had shown any signs of discontent in London, he lost them with the circus. He was a superb performer and a natural-born traveller, but his easy adjustment to the strenuous life was no doubt due to the continuous presence of Matthew Scott, whose hypnotic power over the elephant never wavered. In London, Jumbo's only temper fits occurred when and because Scott was absent, but in America Scott was seldom, if ever, out of Jumbo's sight. He did not even eat with the other circus employees but rather took all his meals with his "Jummie."

They toured with the circus in their own private rail car, which Barnum liked to refer to as "Jumbo's Palace Car." It was an ornate boxcar, painted crimson and gold, with huge double doors in the depressed middle section, giving Jumbo easy access to his travelling home. Scott rode in a bunk near Jumbo's head, and his compartment was separated from the elephant's by a small door, which Jumbo never permitted to be closed for any reason. Whenever Jumbo felt lonely while Scott was sleeping, he would tease and annoy his keeper by groping through the door with his trunk and snatching such small articles as sheets and blankets. Man and beast still shared their daily quart of beer, and the story is told that one night, for some inexplicable reason, Scott forgot to share and guzzled the whole quart himself. Surprised and obviously hurt, Jumbo waited until Scott was fast asleep before reaching through the door with his trunk and picking the rudely awakened Scott right out of his bed and setting him on the floor by the empty bottle. Scott never forgot again.

So it went for two seasons—Jumbo enjoying his new life and Barnum raking in hundreds of thousands of dollars. The show had its traditional Madison Square Garden opening on March 16, and from there it swung through New York, Pennsylvania, New England, and the Maritime Provinces of Canada. After more than a hundred stops covering some eight thousand miles the circus train pulled into the town of St. Thomas, Ontario, in the wee hours of September 15, 1885. As the train rolled into the Grand Trunk Railroad yards east of Woodworth Avenue, it was shifted to a siding.

The main-line track ran in an east-west direction; the siding that held the circus train was to the south of it, separated by only a few feet of gravel roadbed. On the north side of the track was a steep six-foot drop, at the bottom of which was a right-of-way fence and beyond that a vacant field where the big tops would be set up. As the long train stopped on the siding some men uncoupled it near the middle, and the forward part was pulled up a few yards, to make the

CONTINUED ON PAGE 82

"Their huge souls, light as clouds..."

Americans have always loved elephants, perhaps because they embody our national leaning toward the outsized and the grandiose, perhaps simply because they are such unlikely and engaging beasts. James Agee, the brilliant author of A Death in the Family, *shared this love, as is evident in the following excerpt from a letter to his close friend, Episcopal priest Father James Harold Flye. In it he sketches the sad and wistful plot of a possible movie about elephants in America. It was the last letter Agee ever wrote. Before he could mail it, the author died, on May 16, 1955, at the age of forty-six.*

At the beginning, elephants converge from all over Africa, towards a disembodied voice, the voice of God, which addresses them roughly as follows: "My beloved children: you know you are my chosen people. You know that—to you alone—I have given my secret: I do not regard myself as omnipotent. I gave that up when I gave to Man the Will to love me or to hate me, or merely to disregard me. So I can promise you nothing. What little I can tell you is neither encouraging nor discouraging. Your kind is used already for work; and the men who use you are neither markedly improved nor disimproved by contact with you. Nor have you been improved, or disimproved in that process. But now, a new age begins. Soon, now, you will be taken to be *looked upon*, to be regarded as strange and as wonderful and—forgive me, my dear ones—as funny. As I said, I am not omnipotent; I can't even prophesy: I ask only this: be your own good selves, always faithfully, always in knowledge of my love and regard, and through so being, you may convert those heathen, those barbarians, where all else has failed."

During this admonition, and blessing, the oldest elephant sadly leaves the assembly, and walks away to the great, secret, elephant cemetery, and dies there.

Soon after, men come among the elephants, and capture them for circuses.

We move, then, from fiction to fact.

This is what happened; a matter of record; when elephants were brought among civilized men:

1824: The first American circus elephant.

She was bought by a man whose headquarters was at Somers, N. Y. She was called *Old Bet*. She was exhibited locally. In a small town in Western Connecticut, religious people decided that she was the reincarnation of Behemoth, and shot her dead. She was buried at Somers. A statue was raised above her grave. Ever since, it has been a shrine for circus people.

Late 19th Century: Jumbo.

The most famous and beloved of elephants, he died as follows:

He was led across the railroad yards to his private car. A gap was left, in a long line of freight cars, for his crossing. But for this gap, the tracks were hemmed in by linked cars. This was at night. No train was scheduled. But an express came through. Jumbo, seeing it, remembered the gap and turned and ran for it. He ran so hard he overshot it. He turned again, and met the locomotive head-on. He was instantly killed; the locomotive was derailed.

1916: Tennessee: Mary.

In a small Tennessee town—out of what charming provocations you can imagine—Mary went berserk, and killed three men. The general populace decided, accordingly, that she should be hanged. They strung her up to a railroad derrick; she broke it down by sheer weight. They got a stronger derrick: after two hours, Mary died, hanged by the neck, while 5,000 oafs looked on.

1934: Grand Finale.

The greatest choreographer of his time, George Balanchine, instructs the greatest elephant corps of any time, in ballet. The elephants are embarrassed, but dutiful. The big night comes. They dance to music by Stravinsky, in pink tutus. They do very nicely; hardly a mistake. But all through the performance, people roar with joy at their clumsiness, and their dutifulness. The elephants are deeply shamed. Later that night the wisest of them, extending his trunk, licks up a dying cigar-butt, and drops it in fresh straw. All 36 elephants die in the fire. Their huge souls, light as clouds, settle like doves, in the great secret cemetery back in Africa—

And perhaps God speaks, tenderly, again; perhaps saying: "The Peace of God, which passeth all understanding..." etc....

BATTLES OF THE REVOLUTION
TRENTON

A sergeant of the 19th Continental Infantry Regiment   A private of the Fusilier Regiment von Knyphausen

merican spirits were at a low ebb as the year 1776 drew to a close. The Hudson River forts were gone, Long Island and New York were taken, and now Washington's wretched army of three thousand men was in full retreat through New Jersey with Cornwallis' veteran troops close behind. Moreover, the enlistments of many of the Continental soldiers were due to expire with the old year; after December 31 the army would virtually cease to exist. Morale demanded a victory, and if Washington was ever going to strike, it would have to be soon.

A bleak Christmas Day dawned on the American army camped on the Pennsylvania side of the Delaware River. By evening it was blowing a full gale, and the seething river was packed with huge sheets of ice. Nevertheless, twenty-four hundred of Washington's soldiers were clambering into long, shallow boats manned by Colonel John Glover's Marblehead fishermen [see "Soldier in a Longboat," AMERICAN HERITAGE, February, 1960] and setting out for the Jersey shore. Washington was going to attack Trenton, where Colonel Johann Rall and fourteen hundred of his Hessians had gone into winter quarters.

The miserable crossing was completed by three o'clock on the morning of the twenty-sixth, and the men set out on a nine-mile hike over icy roads to Trenton town. They marched through sleet and freezing rain in two columns: Washington and General Nathanael Greene took one along an inland route, and General John Sullivan led the other along the river highway.

At about half past seven, Hessian pickets gaped in astonishment as Greene's troops materialized before their eyes. They raised the alarm, but it was too late; already Sullivan's men were going into action on the other side of town. Sleepy Hessians tumbled out into the streets and tried to form some sort of defense, but the scarecrows in the remnants of Continental uniforms came yelling out of the storm and swept through their ranks. It was a soldier's battle, fought and won piecemeal from street to street and house to house, and it didn't last long. Rall tried to rally his men, failed, and fell mortally wounded. Three quarters of an hour after the fighting started, the defenders laid down their arms and surrendered.

This stunning victory had an immediate effect on the dispirited American people. Washington, whose reputation had suffered greatly during the long months of defeat and retreat, was hailed as a genius, and new recruits turned out to join his revitalized forces. Washington had gambled his army on one bold stroke and, winning, had saved his cause.   —*R.F.S.*

Fourth in a series of paintings for
AMERICAN HERITAGE
BY DON TROIANI

Ragged soldiers of the Continental Army struggle ashore after crossing the ice-choked Delaware in the teeth of a December gale. The imposing figure on the white horse is, of course, General Washington. Members of the Philadelphia Light Horse in their red capes look on at the right of the picture, and the black-coated gunners tend to their piece in the center. The red cockade worn by the horseman

·at the extreme left marks him as a field officer, and the yellow one on the soldier in the foreground shows him to be a captain. The men in their command are ill-clad even by Continental Army standards; some are wearing the remnants of uniforms, others are in sailors' jackets and civilian clothes. The mascot being led by the drummer may well survive the battle only to be eaten at Valley Forge next winter.

"I never have seen Washington so determined"

Captain Andreas Wiederhold,
Hessian forces:

On December 14, 1776, we marched to famous Trenton, which I shall remember as long as I live, and to which place our all too merry Brigadier [Colonel Johann Rall] is said to have brought us by his solicitation. How well he would have done not to have solicited for it! He might perhaps have kept and preserved the undeserved praise which was ignorantly bestowed upon him. But here it all fell into the mud!

. . . .

Major von Dechow very wisely suggested to throw up some earth-works and to put the cannons into them, so that all might be in readiness for as good a defense as possible in the case of an emergency. "Let them come," was the Colonel's answer. "What, earth-works! With the bayonet we will go for them." . . . He believed the very name Rall more effectual and stronger than all the fortifications of Vauban and Coehorn together, and no rebel would have the courage to attack him.

An unknown officer on Washington's staff:

Dec. 23—. . . Washington has just given the counter sign, "Victory or Death." . . . He intends to cross the river, make a ten-mile march to Trenton, and attack Rall just before daybreak. . . .

Dec. 25—Christmas morning. They make a great deal of Christmas in Germany, and no doubt the Hessians will drink a great deal of beer and have a dance to-night. They will be sleepy to-morrow morning. Washington will set the tune for them about daybreak. . . .

Christmas, 6 P.M.—The regiments have had their evening parade, but instead of returning to their quarters are marching toward the ferry. It is fearfully cold and raw and a snow-storm setting in. The wind is northeast and beats in the faces of the men. It will be a terrible night for the soldiers who have no shoes. Some of them have tied old rags around their feet; others are barefoot, but I have not heard a man complain. . . .

Dec. 26, 3 A.M.—I am writing in the ferry house. The troops are all over, and the boats have gone back for the artillery. We are three hours behind the set time. [Colonel John] Glover's men have had a hard time to force the boats through the floating ice with the snow drifting in their faces. I never have seen Washington so determined as he is now. He stands on the bank of the river, wrapped in his cloak, superintending the landing of his troops. He is calm and collected, but very determined. The storm is changing to sleet, and cuts like a knife. The last cannon is being landed, and we are ready to mount our horses.

Private Elisha Bostwick,
Continental Army:

. . . Finally our march began with the torches of our field pieces stuck in the exhalters. [They] sparkled and blazed in the storm all night and about day light a halt was made, at which time his Excellency [Washington] and aids came near to front on the side of the path where the soldiers stood.

I heard his Excellency as he was comeing on speaking to and encourageing the soldiers. The words he spoke as he passed by where I stood and in my hearing were these: "Soldiers, keep by your officers. For God's sake, keep by your officers!" Spoke in a deep and solemn voice.

. . . Our horses were then unharnessed and the artillery men prepared. We marched on and it was not long before we heard the out centries of the enemy both on the road we were in and the eastern road, and their out gards retreated fireing, and our army, then with a quick step . . . entered the town.

Colonel Henry Knox,
Continental Army:

. . . Trenton is an open town, situated nearly on the banks of the Delaware, accessible on all sides. . . . We . . . entered the town . . . pell-mell; and here succeeded a scene of war of which I had often conceived, but never saw before. The hurry, fright, and confusion of the enemy was [not] unlike that which will be when the last trump shall sound. They endeavoured to form in streets, the heads of which we had previously the possession of with cannon and howitzers; these, in the twinkling of an eye, cleared the streets. The backs of the houses were resorted to for shelter. These proved ineffectual: the musketry soon dislodged them. Finally they were driven through the town into an open plain beyond. . . . The poor fellows after they were formed on the plain saw themselves completely surrounded, the only resource left was to force their way through numbers unknown to them. The Hessians lost part of their cannon in the town; they did not relish the project of forcing, and were obliged to surrender upon the spot. . . . It must give a sensible pleasure to every friend of the rights of man to think with how much intrepidity our people pushed the enemy, and prevented their forming in the town.

Colonel Clement Biddle,
Continental Army, to the Committee of Safety:

I have the pleasure to inform you that the Prisoners amount to near one thousand, that their Arms, six brass field pieces, Eight Standards or Colours and a number of Swords, Cartouch Boxes taken in this happy Expedition, are safely arrived at and near this place. If your Honourable Committee could by any means furnish Shoes & Stockings for our Troops it will be a great relief. . . .

I Soldiered With Charlie

Charlie as he looked in uniform

By PHILIP MYERS

Charlie and I first met under the most informal conditions imaginable—we were both stark naked. We were not alone in this, for with hundreds of others we were taking a physical examination for acceptance in the first officers' training camp at Fort Myer, Virginia. The date was May 16, 1917.

On the previous day approximately twenty-five hundred men had descended on the post. Our hopes were high, even though the first latrine rumor most of us heard was that only one in four would be commissioned.

Our company was marched to the post gymnasium early the next morning. Once inside, we were brusquely ordered to strip, then form a single file. It was at this point that the indignities began. As the line entered the first door a hospital corpsman splashed each of us on the chest with a wet sponge. Next another corpsman, armed with an indelible pencil, scrawled a large number on the moist spot for identification. As we passed through a second door, the line never stopping its peristaltic movement, each of us in turn was grabbed by the arm. Some sharp instrument scratched a crosshatching on a spot near the biceps. A damp swab was passed over the lacerated skin, and another vaccination was accomplished.

While we turned our heads to examine our injuries the other arm was seized, and a blunt needle was plunged into it—the first of many, many inoculations. A surprisingly large number of husky men passed out at this point. They were unceremoniously towed out of the way of the procession and propped against the wall, their identifying numbers properly exposed.

Charlie had a huge "35" inscribed on his chest. I followed with a "36." We were becoming acquainted with each other as the snake dance led us through another door. Here our conversation was abruptly interrupted by a newly commissioned lieutenant of the Medical Corps. He practically jumped at Charlie, snapped a question at him, and made rapid notes on his paper-crowded clipboard.

"Thirty-five," he barked, striving hard for the tone of command, "what did you do in civil life?"

"Worked in a bank," Charlie replied with a slight grin.

Perhaps it was the smile that accompanied it, but the answer seemed to infuriate the officer. He glowered at me but without questioning stalked rapidly away.

We came to yet another door. On the far side of it stood the same inquisitor. Spotting Charlie's number, he hurled another question at him.

"Just what did you do in that bank?"

Charlie grinned the infectious smile that I was later to know so well.

"I ran it."

In civilian life a man's mien and clothes give a slight indication of his occupation, but how could anyone even hazard a guess when he was surrounded by hundreds of naked men? Charlie's physique certainly did not suggest the stereotyped banker. Not tall, but powerfully built, he could readily have been taken for a professional athlete. The answer he gave really upset the questioner.

"What bank was it?"

"My bank, you damn fool!"

The astonished doctor hastily scribbled a note on his memo pad, then angrily rushed away. Charlie turned calmly to me and resumed our interrupted conversation. By this time we had discovered many mutual interests and had begun a friendship that was to last for years.

In the meantime the grapevine, starting from the rear of our file of unclad officer-candidates, had passed on the word to be careful how we answered the apparently innocent questions asked of us as we moved through door after door. The inter-

rogation was being conducted, it was said, by psychiatrists, and a wrong answer could mean no commission at all.

Charlie was sure he had muffed his chance and was therefore not at all surprised to be ordered to the base hospital that afternoon for a special examination. Hallucinations! Thinks he owns a bank!

He rejoined the company a few hours later.

"Are you nuts, Charlie?"

"Sure. We're all nuts to be here."

He pitched in with us in the laborious task of issuing uniforms and equipment. With both arms painfully damaged by the morning's experience, this turned out to be real, unrelenting hard work for bodies unaccustomed to such physical exertion. Taps came at eleven o'clock, but we were kept at it until the job was done to the company commander's satisfaction. Our second night in the army was notably short. Reveille found us up and in line, if not awake, before dawn.

Charlie and I were of about the same height, and thus we were placed in the same squad. He was thirty-one, ten years older than I and infinitely more sophisticated. It was fascinating and informative to get him talking when opportunity offered.

One such occasion was the night we spent on a minor tactics problem in the surrounding Virginia woods. Our squad had been designated as support to a line of outposts. We spread our blankets for protection against the voracious mosquitoes and lay on the ground near a towering pine. Sleep was out of the question despite a strenuous day in the field. The pungent smell of moist earth filled our nostrils. Fireflies made a fairyland of our little glade. Overhead we looked into the infinity of brilliant stars. We forgot Kaiser Bill and the war we were trying to enter with a bar on each shoulder.

All was quiet until a muted voice was heard.

"Charlie, were you ever in love?"

That started it. The pale streaks of dawn were visible before this most memorable bull session ended. There was no hint of boasting in Charlie's answer. We, the younger and inexperienced ones, listened and learned from one who had known life at its fullest.

Toward the end of the gestation period for us ninety-day wonders the weeding-out process was begun. The high command devised a really practical test to determine possible fitness for line officers. Our company was divided into two segments. One half was stationed on one side of the parade ground. On the opposite side was the other. In between was a group of regular officers to act as judges. A man from each section was called upon to give three consecutive commands to the distant group. The promptness of response was the test of the carrying power of the candidate's voice.

Charlie's voice was weak. There was scant chance that the distant platoon would even hear, let alone understand, him. But when it was his turn, he stepped out of ranks, faced the wide expanse of parade ground, tried to let out a yell, and stamped his foot. Immediately the faraway group executed a snappy right shoulder arms. Charlie took a deep breath, emitted a shallow bellow, and again stamped his foot. Just as promptly, order arms was performed. Once again the deep inhalation, the order, and the stamped foot. This time the officers in midfield saw present arms beautifully achieved.

They looked askance at one another. To them Charlie's orders had sounded nothing at all like the words employed in infantry drill regulations. And yet the platoon opposite had obeyed him as one man.

Charlie passed the test. He was popular with the entire company, and of course the sequence from the manual was a prearranged hoax. Stamping his foot was the signal for the men to go through the drill.

Graduation day was set for August 15. On the Saturday before that date I had received a pass and made my way to Washington. Only a few of the more obvious misfits had been sent back to civilian life, but the latest rumor had it that the coming week would witness the departure of hundreds of borderline cases. The suspense was almost unbearable.

My purpose in going to the capital was to visit Fred Essary, Washington correspondent for the Baltimore *Sun*, in his office on Fourteenth Street. He, I felt sure, would have a release giving the names of the successful candidates.

As a former reporter, I had a press card that served as a proper introduction to him. Yes, he had the list, but it was not to be made public until the fifteenth. Then he rose from the chair behind his flattop desk, looked sternly at me, and said: "There is something that I must do right now in my back office. It will take me no less than five minutes. I never lock the top right-hand drawer of my desk."

At the door he paused and added with a grin: "For heaven's sake, don't tell anybody else except the men in your own squad."

On the lightest of feet, despite the heavy garrison shoes in which they were encased, I made my way to the military shops that lined the avenue. There I purchased that silent mark of rank, a pair of leather puttees, was fitted by a tailor for a uniform with braid on the sleeves, and bought other such things as befitted a new shave-tail. I had made the grade. So had Charlie. In all, seven of our closely knit squad had been awarded commissions.

Back at Fort Myer again, I quietly passed on my good news where it applied. It was received with prop-erly restrained enthusiasm. Somehow or other the seven of us wangled passes to the city, where the others first made purchases such as mine; then at the insistence of Charlie we met at the Shoreham Hotel. He celebrated his and our good fortune by having us as his guests. The rest of that evening, and indeed of the ensuing week, is a blurred but happy memory.

Only one who knows the workings of the military mind could explain the assignment of us fledglings. Of our squad only Charlie and I were ordered to report to the Commanding Officer, 319th Infantry, at Camp Lee, Virginia.

We arrived at an unfinished building complex and were quartered in what was to be a company barracks. It lacked sash in the windows, but it did have a rainproof roof. No running water was available. We had to walk almost a mile for mess three times a day.

By the third day our chins began to look like today's hippies'. Coca-Cola, the ubiquitous, was plentiful, so we did not thirst, but, oh, for the comfort of a shave. Charlie, more resourceful than most of us, attempted, without too much success, to work up a lather using the Coke. At least it wet his beard and enabled him to hack his way through it with his straight razor. The bubbles tickled, and the stickiness persisted afterward; still, we all followed his suggestion and once again looked more like officers.

Jitney service to Petersburg was somewhat less than satisfactory, so one day Charlie appeared with a Hudson touring car, the use of which he shared freely with anyone off duty. The mysterious workings of the mili-tary mind again showed shortly after Thanksgiving. Camp Lee was assuming some semblance of order when Charlie was suddenly transferred to the Air Corps. He left the key in his car with the quiet remark "Somebody will want to use it."

I did not see him at all during the hostilities. It was not until a reunion of the surviving officers of the 319th was held in Washington about ten years later that we met again. It was at that banquet that each of us was called upon to relate an incident under the heading "Do you remember when. . . ."

With Charlie sitting at my side, I told of the time in the Fort Myer gymnasium when he had told his inquisitor he owned a bank. One of those present, unfamiliar with the story and not knowing anything about the man involved, naively asked him, "Did you? What was the bank?"

"Well, it wasn't just exactly a bank," Charlie explained. "It was a financial institution, though. It is called Merrill Lynch, Pierce, Fenner and Beane. You may have heard of it."

Although from time to time we exchanged letters recalling the days when we soldiered together, I never saw him again. Charles Edward Merrill, my friend Charlie, died on October 6, 1956.

Philip Myers, a retired manufacturer of architectural millwork, has for over a half century devoted his spare time to writing. His first article appeared in Munsey's Magazine *in 1917.*

PHOTO CREDIT: MERRILL LYNCH, PIERCE, FENNER & SMITH INC.

COLLECTION OF E. M. HALLIDAY

The Unexpected Mrs. Stowe

CONTINUED FROM PAGE 9

die, with no way to help, she said, no way even to ease his suffering.

Calvin returned to her very soon after that, determined to leave Cincinnati for good. He had accepted a professorship at Bowdoin College, in Brunswick, Maine, and before he could settle up his affairs in Cincinnati, he characteristically sent Harriet and three of the children off to Maine ahead of him.

She left Cincinnati in the early spring of 1850, a shabby little figure, perfectly erect, perhaps no more than five feet tall, nearly forty, and pregnant once again. She boarded a riverboat at the foot of town, saying farewell with no misgivings. She was going home, she felt.

She was also heading for a sudden and colossal notoriety of a kind never known by any American woman before, and very few since; but of that she had no notion whatever. Nor did she or anyone else alive have any idea how important those seventeen years in Cincinnati had been to her and, as things turned out, to the whole course of American history.

She sailed up the Ohio to Pittsburgh, where she changed to a canal-boat. Already she was feeling so good she got out and walked the towpath between locks. At Johnstown the boat and all its passengers were hoisted up and over the Allegheny Mountains by that thrilling mechanical contrivance of the nineteenth century, the Portage Railroad. East of the mountains she went by rail to New York and there crossed by ferry to Brooklyn to see her younger brother, Henry Ward, pastor of Plymouth Church. As children they had sometimes been taken for twins, only Henry Ward had been thick of speech and considered the slow one. Now she took note of his obvious success, and they went out for a drive in a spotless six-hundred-dollar car-

riage, a recent gift from his parishioners.

In a few days she went on to Hartford, still looking after the children and all their baggage. Her spirits were soaring. At Hartford she stayed with her sisters Mary and Isabella; in Boston with her brother Edward, who was growing ever more militant over the slavery issue. All the Beechers were growing more militant over one thing or another. For Isabella it was women's rights; for the brilliant Catherine, education; for Charles, freedom from theological authority. From Boston, Harriet took the Bath Steamer to Maine, sailing headlong into a northeaster.

On the day they were scheduled to arrive at Brunswick, one story goes, the president of Bowdoin sent a professor named Smith down to greet the new faculty wife, but Smith returned disappointed, saying she must have been delayed. Nobody got off the boat, he said, except an old Irish woman and her brats.

Brunswick offered precious few of the eastern civilities Mrs. Stowe had longed for, and the house Calvin had taken in advance turned out to be deserted, dreary, and damp, to use her words. She went straight to work, refinishing floors, putting up wallpaper—the pioneer again. When Calvin wrote from Cincinnati to say he was sick and plainly dying and that she and theirs would soon be plunged into everlasting debt, she read the letter with humor and stuffed it into the stove.

Calvin showed up before summer, her baby was born, she rested two weeks. When winter came, there were holes in her shoes, and the house was so cold during one long storm that the children had trouble sitting still long enough to eat their meals. They were living on $1,700 a year. It was during the following spring

that she began *Uncle Tom's Cabin.*

People are still trying to interpret the book and to explain just how and why she came to write it. At first she said she really didn't write it at all. She said the book came to her in visions and all she did was write down what she saw. When someone reproached her for letting Little Eva die, she answered, "Why, I could not help it. I felt as badly as anyone could! It was like a death in my own family and it affected me so deeply that I could not write a word for two weeks after her death.". Years later she stated categorically, "God wrote it." And a great many of her readers were quite willing to let it go at that.

The truth is, the subject of the book had been all around her for a very long time. Old Lyman had been able to make Litchfield farmers weep when he preached on slavery. In Cincinnati she had opened her own Sunday school to black children, and the Lane Seminary had been a hotbed of abolitionist fervor. The Underground Railroad, she later claimed, went directly through her Cincinnati house, which was a bit of an exaggeration; but on one occasion Calvin and her brother Charles did indeed help a black woman and her child elude a slave hunter. The only time she was in an actual slave state, during a visit across the Ohio River in Kentucky, she made no show of emotion about it. But stories she heard from the Negro women she knew in Cincinnati moved her enormously, particularly those told by a gentle person named Eliza Buck, who helped her with housework and whose children, Harriet Stowe discovered with incredulity, had all been fathered by the woman's former master in Kentucky. "You know, Mrs. Stowe," she had said, "slave women cannot help themselves."

Eliza Buck told her of lashings and of Negro families split up and "sold down the river." Once on an Ohio River wharf Mrs. Stowe had seen with her own eyes a husband and wife torn apart by a slave trader.

By the time she came east to Maine, Henry Ward was using his Brooklyn pulpit to raise money to buy children out of slavery. In Boston she and Edward had talked long and emotionally about the Fugitive Slave Bill, then being debated in Congress, which made it a federal crime to harbor or assist the escaped "property" of a slave master. Her duty was plain. There was, she said, a standard higher than an act of Congress.

She did some research in Boston and corresponded with Frederick Douglass on certain details. But for all that, the book would be written more out of something within her, something she knew herself about bondage and the craving for liberation, than from any documentary sources or personal investigation of Negro slavery in the South. Indeed she really knew very little about Negro slavery in the South. Her critics would be vicious with her for this, of course, and she would go so far as to write a whole second book in defense of her sources. But *Uncle Tom's Cabin* could never be accounted for that way.

There is probably something to the story that she began the book as a result of a letter from Edward's wife. "Hattie," wrote her sister-in-law from Boston, "if I could use the pen as you can, I would write something that will make this whole nation feel what an accursed thing slavery is." To which Hattie answered, "As long as the baby sleeps with me nights, I can't do much at anything, but I will do it at last. I will write that thing if I live."

The story appeared first as a serial in the *National Era,* an antislavery paper, beginning in June, 1851. It took her a year to write it all, and apparently she did Uncle Tom's death scene first and at a single sitting, writing on brown wrapping paper when her writing paper ran out. The finished story was brought out in book form by the publisher, John P. Jewett, in two volumes on March 20, 1852, a month before the serialized version ended.

Calvin thought the book had little importance. He wept over it, but he wept over most of the things she wrote. Her publisher warned that her subject was unpopular and said she took too long to tell her story. On the advice of a friend who had not read the manuscript, she decided to take a 10 per cent royalty on every copy sold instead of a fifty-fifty division of profit or losses, as had also been offered to her.

She herself expected to make no money from it; she thought it inadequate and was sure her friends would be disappointed with her. Within a week after publication ten thousand copies had been sold. The publisher had three power presses running twenty-four hours a day. In a year sales in the United States came to more than three hundred thousand. The book made publishing history right from the start. In England, where Mrs. Stowe had no copyright and therefore received no royalties, sales were even more stupendous. A million and a half copies were sold in about a year's time. The book appeared in thirty-seven different languages. "It is no longer permissible to those who can read not to have read it," wrote George Sand from France, who said Mrs. Stowe had no talent, only genius, and called her a saint.

The book had a strange power over almost everyone who read it then, and for all its Victorian mannerisms and frequent patches of sentimentality much of still does. Its characters have a vitality of a kind comparable to the most memorable figures in literature. There is sweep and power to the narrative, and there are scenes that once read are not forgotten. The book is also rather different from what most people imagine, largely because it was eventually eclipsed by the stage version, which Mrs. Stowe had nothing to do with (and from which she never received a cent) and which was probably performed more often than any play in the language, evolving after a few years into something between circus and minstrel show. (One successful road company advertised ". . . a pack of genuine bloodhounds; two Toppsies; Two Marks, Eva and her Pony 'Prince'; African Mandolin Players; 'Tinker' the famous Trick Donkey.") In the book, for example, no bloodhounds chase Eliza and her baby across the ice.

What the book did at the time was to bring slavery out into the open and show it for what it was, in human terms. No writer had done that before. Slavery had been argued over in the abstract, preached against as a moral issue, its evils whispered about in polite company. But the book made people at that time *feel* what slavery was about. ("The soul of eloquence is feeling," old Lyman had written.)

Moreover, Harriet Stowe had made a black man her hero, and she took his race seriously, and no American writer had done that before.

The fundamental fault, she fervently held, was with the system. Every white American was guilty, the Northerner no less than the slaveholder, especially the church-going kind, *her* kind. Simon Legree, it should perhaps always be remembered, was a Vermonter.

That Uncle Tom would one day be used as a term of derision ("A Negro who is held to be humiliatingly subservient or deferential to whites," according to the *American Heritage Dictionary*) she would have found impossible to fathom, and heartbreaking. For her he was something very close to a black Christ. He is the one character in all her book who lives, quite literally, by the Christian ideal. And if one has doubts that she could see black as beautiful or that she saw emancipation for the black man as a chance for full manhood and dignity, there is her description of Eliza's husband, George Harris, as straight-backed, confident, "his face settled and resolute." When George and his family, having escaped into Ohio, are cornered by slave hunters, Mrs. Stowe writes a scene in which George is fully prepared to kill his tormentors and to die himself rather than permit his wife and son to be taken back into slavery. ". . . I am a free man, standing on God's free soil," George yells from the rock ledge to which he has retreated, "and my wife and my child I claim as mine. . . . We have arms to defend ourselves and we mean to do it. You can come up if you like; but the first one of you that comes within the range of our bullets is a dead man, and the next, and the next, and so on till the last."

She seems to have been everywhere at once after the book was published —Hartford, New Haven, Brooklyn, Boston. Almost immediately the South began boiling with indignation. She was a radical, it was said. All the Beechers were radicals. She began receiving threatening letters from the South, and once Calvin unwrapped a small parcel addressed to her to find a human ear that had been severed from the head of a black slave. Calvin grew more and more distraught. They decided it was time to move again, now to Andover, Massachusetts, to take up a previously offered teaching job at the seminary there.

Then they were sailing to England, where huge crowds waited for her at railroad stations, hymns were composed in her honor, children came up to her carriage with flowers. She went about in a gray cloak carrying a paint box. She was a tireless tourist. And she worried. "The power of fictitious writing, for good as well as evil is a thing which ought most seriously to be reflected on. No one can fail to see that in our day it is becoming a very great agency."

When war came, everyone told her it was her war, and she thought so too. In South Carolina, as the war commenced, the wife of a plantation owner wrote in her diary that naturally slavery had to go, but added, "Yes, how I envy those saintly Yankee women, in their clean cool New England homes, writing to make their fortunes and to shame us."

Harriet Stowe never saw the Civil War as anything but a war to end slavery, and all her old Beecher pacifist principles went right out the window. "Better, a thousand times better, open, manly, energetic war, than cowardly and treacherous peace," she proclaimed. Her oldest son, Frederick, put on a uniform and went off to fight. Impatient with Lincoln for not announcing emancipation right away, she went down to Washington when he finally proclaimed that the slaves would be free, and was received privately in the White House. The scene is part of our folklore. "So this is the little woman who made this big war," Lincoln is supposed to have said as he shook her hand.

She was sitting in the gallery at the Boston Music Hall, attending a concert, on January 1, 1863, the day the Emancipation Proclamation became effective. When an announcement of the historic event was made from the stage, somebody called out that she was in the gallery. In an instant the audience was on its feet cheering while she stood and bowed, her bonnet awry.

After the war she kept on writing. In fact, as is sometimes overlooked, that is what Harriet Beecher Stowe was, a writer, and one of the most industrious we have ever had. Unwittingly she had written the abolitionist manifesto, although she did not consider herself an abolitionist. She agreed with her father that abolitionists "were like men who would burn down their houses to get rid of the rats." She was not a crusader pure and simple. She never considered

herself an extremist, and she seldom took an extreme position on any issue. She was a reformer, and there was an evangelical undercurrent to just about everything she wrote. But writing was her work, her way to make herself useful.

Her life was about half over when she wrote *Uncle Tom's Cabin,* but for thirty years more she wrote almost a book a year on the average, plus innumerable essays, poems, children's stories, and magazine articles, many of which she did under the pseudonym Christopher Crowfield. Perhaps her most artful novel, *The Minister's Wooing,* ran to fifty printings, and a magazine article, "The True Story of Lady Byron's Life," which appeared in the *Atlantic Monthly* in 1869, caused more furor than anything published in America since *Uncle Tom's Cabin.*

During a second visit to England she had become fast friends with the widow of Lord Byron, who confided the terrible secret that the great Byron had committed incest with his half sister and that a child had been born as a result. Mrs. Stowe kept the secret for thirteen years, but when Byron's former mistress, Countess Guiccioli, published her memoirs and portrayed Lady Byron as a self-righteous tyrant who would drive any mortal male to excesses, Harriet Stowe decided it was time to strike a blow in her friend's behalf, Lady Byron by this time having been dead for nearly a decade. So she told the whole story.

All kinds of accusations were hurled at her, some quite unpleasant. She rode out the storm, however, and again, as with *Uncle Tom,* she wrote a book to justify what she had written. But her standing with the American public would never be the same.

She could write in all kinds of places, under every kind of condition. She was always bothered by deadlines, and it seems she was always in need of money. The royalties poured in, but the more she had the more she spent—on a huge Gothic villa in

Hartford that was all gables and turrets and was never finished completely; on a cotton plantation in Florida where she intended to provide Negroes with a program of work and education; and later, when that failed, on an orange and lemon grove at Mandarin, Florida, "where the world is not," she said, and where she hoped her unfortunate son Frederick might find himself.

Frederick had trouble staying sober. His problem had started before the war, but at Gettysburg he had been hit in the head by a shell fragment, and, his mother would always believe, he had never been himself again. "After that," one of her grandsons would write, "he not only was made drunk by the slightest amount of alcohol but he could not resist taking it."

Calvin grew enormously fat, ever more distant, and of even less use than before when it came to the everyday details of life. Moreover, Harriet found fame increasingly difficult. She had become a national institution. Her correspondence alone would have drained a less vigorous spirit.

Tragedy struck repeatedly. In 1857, upon returning from Europe, she learned that her son Henry, a student at Dartmouth, had drowned while swimming in the Connecticut River. In 1870 Frederick, unable to endure his mother's Florida experiment any longer, wrote her a touching apology and went to sea, shipping around the Horn. It is known that he got as far as San Francisco, but after that he disappeared and was never heard from again. She would go to her grave with every confidence that he would return one day.

But it was the Brooklyn scandal that hurt her worst of all, she said. In November of 1872 a New York paper reported that her beloved brother Henry Ward, by then the most popular preacher in America, had been carrying on an adulterous affair with one of his parishioners. His enemies swept in for the kill. For all the Beechers the gossip was agonizing. A sensational trial resulted, the husband bringing suit against Beecher for alienation of his wife's affections. It dragged on for six months and was the talk of the country. Whether Beecher was guilty or innocent was never proved one way or the other. He denied everything, the jury was unable to agree on a verdict, and as far as his sister was concerned his character was never even in question.

The whole story was a slanderous fabrication, she said, and she stood by him through the entire grisly, drawn-out business, as did all the Beechers except Isabella Beecher Hooker, who was only a half sister, it was noted, and was regarded by many as just a little unbalanced. (Isabella, who called herself "the inspired one," wanted to take charge of a service at Plymouth Church herself and "as one commissioned from on high" declare her brother's guilt from his own pulpit. Years later, when he was dying, she even tried to force her way into his house to get a deathbed confession.)

But it would be mistaken to suggest that Harriet's life became increasingly burdensome. Quite the contrary. As time passed she seems to have grown ever more liberated from her past. She drew further and further from the shadow of her harsh Calvinist heritage, eventually rejecting it altogether. She had long since discarded the doctrine of original sin. Neither man nor nature was necessarily corrupt, she now held. Hers was a faith of love and Christian charity. She had a seemingly limitless love for the whole human family. Years before, Catherine, her spinster sister, had been the first of the Beechers to rebel against the traditional faith when a young man she was engaged to marry, a gifted Yale professor of philosophy, was lost at sea and Catherine had had to face the terrible Calvinist conclusion that the young man was consigned to eternal damnation because he had never repented. In time all of Lyman Beecher's offspring would desert the faith. Henry Ward would even go so far as to preach that there is no hell.

For Harriet, Calvinism was repugnant, a "glacial" doctrine, although she admired enormously the fervor it had given the Puritan colonists of her native New England and the solid purpose and coherence of the communities they established. Like many of her time she sorely lamented the decline of Christian faith in the land. It was the root of the breakdown of the old order, she believed. Mostly, it seems, she admired the backbone the old religion gave people. "They who had faced eternal ruin with an unflinching gaze," she wrote, "were not likely to shrink before the comparatively trivial losses and gains of any mere earthly conflict." If she herself could not accept the articles of the Puritan faith, she seemed to wish everybody else would. And once from Florida she wrote: ". . . never did we have a more delicious spring. I never knew such altogether perfect weather. It is enough to make a saint out of the toughest old Calvinist that ever set his face as a flint. How do you think New England theology would have fared, if our fathers had landed here instead of on Plymouth Rock?"

Like numerous other literary figures of the day she tried spiritualism and claimed that her son Henry had returned from somewhere beyond to pluck a guitar string for her. She became an Episcopalian, and she developed an open fondness for such things as Europe (Paris and Italy especially), Rubens, elegant society, and Florida, in particular Florida (". . . this wild, wonderful, bright, and vivid growth, that is all new, strange and unknown by name to me . . ."). The theatre and dancing were no longer viewed as sinful. She rejected the idea that "there was something radically corrupt and

Sitting by a portrait of her brother Henry Ward Beecher, Mrs. Stowe, at eighty-two, was photographed in her Hartford home.
STOWE-DAY FOUNDATION

wicked in the body and in the physical system." She took a little claret now on occasion. An account of a visit to Portsmouth, New Hampshire, suggests that once at least she may have taken a little too much claret.

She was asked to give readings, to go on the lyceum, as the contemporary lecture circuit was called, like Robert Ingersoll, P. T. Barnum, and the feminists. She needed the money, so at age sixty-one, having never made a public speech before, she embarked on a new career with its endless train rides, bad food, and dreary hotels. She was very shy at first and not much good at it. But she got over that and in time became quite accomplished. "Her performance could hardly be called a reading," reported the Pittsburgh *Gazette*, "it was recitative and she seldom glanced at the book. Her voice betrayed the veritable Yankee twang. . . . Her voice is low, just tinged in the slightest with huskiness, but is quite musical. In manner she was vivacious and gave life to many of the pages, more by suggestive action than by utterances. . . . She seemed perfectly possessed on the stage, and read with easy grace. . . ."

She found she could move her audiences to great emotional heights, but to laughter especially. And she loved the life. Her health picked up. "I never sleep better than after a long day's ride," she wrote.

Her appearance never changed much. She put on no new airs. Nothing, in fact, good or bad, seemed capable of changing that plain, earnest, often whimsical manner. She acquired a number of new friendships that meant a great deal to her, with Oliver Wendell Holmes and Mark Twain particularly. Henry Drummond, the noted Scottish religious writer, wrote, after a visit to Hartford: "Next door to Twain I found Mrs. Harriet Beecher Stowe, a wonderfully agile old lady, as fresh as a squirrel still, but with the face and air of a lion." And he concluded: "I have not been so taken with any one on this side of the Atlantic."

Her affections for Calvin seem to have grown stronger, if anything. He had become absorbed in Semitic studies, let his beard grow, and took to wearing a skullcap. She began calling him "My Old Rabbi." His apparitions took up more and more of his time, and for a while he was having nightly encounters with the Devil, who came on horseback, Calvin said. But otherwise his mind stayed quick and clear until the end, and she found him exceedingly good company.

In their last years they seem also to have had few financial worries. Among other things a book of his, *The Origin and History of the Books of the Bible*, had a surprisingly large sale. And their affairs in general were being capably managed by their twin daughters, Eliza and Harriet, maiden ladies who apparently had considerable "faculty."

Calvin died peacefully enough, with Harriet at his bedside, on August 6, 1886. She lived on for another ten years, slipping off ever so gradually into a gentle senility.

In a letter to Oliver Wendell Holmes she wrote: "I make no mental effort of any sort; my brain is tired out. It was a woman's brain and not a man's, and finally from sheer fatigue and exhaustion in the march and strife of life it gave out before the end was reached. And now I rest me, like a moored boat, rising and falling on the water, with loosened cordage and flapping sail."

She was eighty-two. She spent hours looking at picture books, bothering no one, or went out gathering flowers, "a tiny withered figure in a garden hat," as one writer described her. On occasion she took long walks beside the river, an Irish nurse generally keeping her company. Sometimes, Mark Twain would recall, she "would slip up behind a person who was deep in dreams and musings and fetch a war whoop that would jump that person out of his clothes."

And every now and then, during moments of astonishing clarity, she would talk again about *Uncle Tom's Cabin,* the book that had just "come" to her in visions. Once, years earlier, when she was having trouble writing, she had said: "If there had been a grand preparatory blast of trumpets or had it been announced that Mrs. Stowe would do this or that, I think it likely I could not have written; but nobody expected anything . . . and so I wrote freely."

She died near midnight on July 1, 1896.

David McCullough, whose most recent book, The Great Bridge, *was a best seller, is now at work on a history of the Panama Canal, a subject he wrote about for* AMERICAN HERITAGE *in his article "A Man, a Plan, a Canal, Panama!" (June, 1971).*

In This Proud Land

CONTINUED FROM PAGE 55

pictures which showed prosperity and timelessness. . . .

"But the faces to me were the most significant part of the file. I remember when [John] Steinbeck came in and looked at the pictures for a couple of days. Those tragic, beautiful faces were what inspired him to write *The Grapes of Wrath*. He caught in words everything the photographers were trying to say in pictures."

The faces that so gripped Stryker made him more and more curious about the small towns, the places where the faces lived. His staff, by then used to Stryker's shooting scripts, began to receive long lists of questions about towns, such as:

What do people do at home in the evenings?

Do the activities in a small town differ from those in a large city?

Do they vary according to income groups?

How do various income levels dress when they go to church?

Where do people meet?

Do beer halls and pool halls take the place of country clubs for the poor?

Has anyone ever taken a really good series of pictures of a filling station, showing its relationship to the restless, shifting American population?

The shift in Stryker's direction had far-reaching results. For not only did the Historical Section of the FSA move beyond its original role as a propaganda agency, but the new, broad, and positive view of America that the photographers were recording was hungrily grabbed up by news agencies and magazines throughout the country. A new outlook and sophistication gripped the photographers who had worked so long with rural people. They began to function as reporters, feeding back to Stryker graphic descriptions of when and where unrest and injustice were

building up. And he in turn would see that the information worked its way into the right channels for government action. He once remarked, "This was all part of our job to record contemporary history. That's why I was once startled—though not displeased—when someone called me 'a press agent of the underprivileged.'"

Press agent though he might have been, Stryker was also a watchdog of the national image. One day, shortly before the Germans launched their attack in Europe, a well-dressed gentleman from the German embassy showed up at Stryker's office, asking to be shown the "famous" pictures of America—the sharecroppers and migrants, floods and dust storms, and other scenes of woe and misery that had been printed across America. Stryker recalled: "He was a very pleasant little Nazi. I had no intention of allowing the records of America's internal problems to fall into his hands. I had the file clerks show him a wonderful range of things—mountains and rivers and lush fields, well-dressed people living off what fat there was left of the land. He left without having chosen a single one."

Up to December 7, 1941, the well-established Historical Section pretty much had carte blanche in covering America's prewar build-up as Stryker wanted it done. But after Pearl Harbor bureaucratic changes, a cutback in funds, and a congressional assault on the FSA wiped out all hopes that Stryker had for a meaningful study of America emerging as the major world power. For nearly two years he fought to keep the project alive, sending photographers into the field to gather some of the most poignant shots to come out of the section. But in September, 1943, Stryker gave up and resigned.

Speaking of his days at Farm Secu-

rity, Stryker once remarked, "The pictures were the important thing. To spend all that money [nearly a million dollars] to get all those pictures [nearly 270,000] was something of a bureaucratic miracle. Toward the end there was strong pressure from the government to destroy the entire file, negatives included. For a time it looked like everything would be lost. Then my old friend Archibald MacLeish appeared as head of the Library of Congress. I had always wanted the collection to go there, and so it did, narrowed down to 170,000 negatives."

Of the seventy thousand pictures on file at the Library of Congress an estimated forty thousand are of agricultural programs, dedications, and the war effort. The discrepancy between the seventy thousand file prints and the 170,000 negatives is, for the most part, duplication of subject material. Of the 270,000 photographs actually taken during the project's lifetime, Stryker killed—by punching holes in the negatives—about a hundred thousand that he considered inferior.

The FSA photo project was unique. Not only were the times and people right, but Roy Stryker was certainly right. Asked once whether there could ever again be such a project, Stryker replied, "It was all just a little like the process of evolution that I learned about years ago at the Colorado School of Mines. When the water temperature was right, when the salts in the river were right, the salamanders came out of the water, and pretty soon human beings were created. Now, do you know what the water temperature down in Washington is? Do you know if the salts are right? Well, don't come out of the water until you do."

Then he added, "Farm Security was one of those freaks, one of those salamanders. It can't happen again. But something new will happen. Something different. I wish to hell I could be around for it." ☆

Jumbo CONTINUED FROM PAGE 68

unloading (and later the loading) of the animals faster by eliminating the long walk around the end of the train. Everything seemed routine.

Halfway through the night show the elephants performed their usual "military drill," after which, according to set routine, twenty-nine of them were to be taken back to the train and loaded for the trip to the next town. Fred R. Armes, the operator in charge of the Grand Trunk Railroad depot at St. Thomas that night, requested (or so it was later claimed) the circus men not to begin loading the elephants until 9:55 that night, long after a westbound express freight was due to pass through. Even then they were to wait for a yard crew and, as still another precaution, to use a designated crossing, far up the track by the station. But the impatient elephant handlers tore down a section of right-of-way fence directly between the huge tents and the circus train and proceeded early in the evening to march the elephants up the embankment, across the main-line track, and into their cars.

This left two of the show's elephants unloaded: the smallest, a dwarf clown elephant named Tom Thumb, and the largest, the towering Jumbo. They had been used to close the act, and it was about eight fifteen when Scott led the elephants through the dismantled fence and up the embankment and walked eastward with them down the main track to the waiting cars.

At about the same time the Grand Trunk's Special Freight #151 was nearing the St. Thomas rail yard, pulled by high-wheeled, diamond-stacked locomotive #88. It was not scheduled to stop in St. Thomas, and as it neared the rail yard it entered a downgrade and gained speed. To engineer William Burnip everything was going routinely. But as he scanned the track ahead he saw—or thought he saw, in the pitifully weak light of the kerosene lamp above the cowcatcher—a hulking gray silhouette, a shade lighter than the surrounding night, looming over the rails.

As the train roared closer Burnip, thunderstruck, dimly perceived not one blur but two—*elephants,* plodding toward him! Reacting frantically, he lunged for the Johnson bar, throwing the engine mechanism into reverse, and blew three short blasts on the whistle for brakes. It was two years before the installation of the Westinghouse air brake, so all the braking had to be done manually by the brakeman, who turned the great handwheels at the end of each boxcar. Slowly, car by car, the wheels locked with a banshee screech, shooting glowing sparks high in the air, as did the high wheels of the locomotive, now churning backward as the engine reversed itself. But Burnip must have known the situation was hopeless. The feeble head-lamp had not reflected the dull gray hides of the elephants until it was too late, and moreover the train was still gaining speed on the downgrade. Seeing that collision was absolutely inevitable, Burnip and his fireman could do nothing but save themselves, and they leaped from the cab at the last instant.

For Scott and the two elephants it was a long walk back up the track to the Palace Car, and just as they were opposite the flagman Scott's ears picked up the shriek of a train whistle—three short blasts that meant emergency brakes. At once he turned to the flagman: "What line is that train on?" he demanded.

The flagman stood stiff with horror: "My God, it's on our track!" The dim kerosene lamp became visible, the rumble more audible, and the flagman, recovering, began to sprint toward it, waving his lantern desperately. Exactly what happened next is, to the present day, not definitely known, and several totally irreconcilable versions have been published.

Some forty years later a Barnum and Bailey circus clown with a fine sense of the dramatic said that Jumbo stood his ground, facing the oncoming freight, bellowing with rage. "I happen to know," he wrote, "that Jumbo was a big, obstinate brute, and was killed by his refusal to get out of the way of a fast freight." The depot master, Fred Armes, in another version of the story, had the irascible and stupid Jumbo charging the oncoming express freight, trumpeting in anger, trying to knock it off the tracks. But his account appeared when Barnum was suing the Grand Trunk line for a hundred thousand dollars, and the road's officials had ample time to remind Armes that the fastest way to absolve the company of guilt in the accident would be to say that Jumbo had thundered into a vicious, unprovoked charge at the innocent freight train. P. T. Barnum's own account was full of splendid exaggeration. But what actually happened, as far as can be determined, was unromantic.

Scott, nearly in tears from fright, shouting "Run, Jumbo, run!" managed to turn the elephants around on the track; and Jumbo, sensing the danger he was in, set off down the track as fast as he could, waving his trunk in the air, roaring and screeching as he had never done in his life. Tom Thumb, the clown elephant, followed Scott and Jumbo at his best

speed, but Jumbo's long legs soon outdistanced the little dwarf, and he fell rapidly behind. Scott was running beside Jumbo, desperately urging the beast to run down the steep embankment to safety, but Jumbo refused to try it. Instead he tried instinctively to outdistance the train, but sadly for him elephants are incapable of genuine running—they can only walk fast—so he was doomed to lose.

Scott saw that there was no chance of reaching the end of the circus train and ducking behind it—the express would catch them long before that. But there was the break where two cars had been uncoupled to let the animals pass through. Yes, the break! If he could get Jumbo to stop and turn through the break, it would be all right; it wasn't far ahead. When they were at last a bare three car lengths from the narrow opening, the speeding express freight crashed into Tom Thumb, who had been lagging farther and farther behind. The cowcatcher caught him low on the hind legs and spun him off the track, down the embankment into a telephone pole and finally into a fence, with a broken leg.

When Jumbo and Scott finally reached the breach, Scott stopped and called at the top of his lungs to the madly trumpeting Jumbo to fol-

low him through the break, but the seven-ton animal's tremendous momentum carried him two cars past the opening before he understood and could stop to turn. Just as he stopped and before he could turn around, the locomotive slammed into his backside. Jumbo went to his knees, and the train skidded off the rails with such driving force that it shoved him violently under the heavy iron wheel-carriage of a circus car, pulverizing the massive skull and driving a tusk back into his brain.

Burnip and his fireman picked themselves up from the ground, badly shaken but not seriously injured. Some circus men pulled the crippled Tom Thumb to his feet and helped him down the track. He would live, though he would limp for the rest of his days.

Scott was stunned as he approached the crumpled body of his companion of twenty years. Jumbo was still conscious. When Scott crawled under the car by the huge, lacerated head to comfort the groaning animal, Jumbo took his hand in his trunk, as if he understood, and died quietly. Scott wept unashamedly. A large crowd had gathered, and when Jumbo ceased breathing, Scott was gently pulled away. A hundred sixty men, straining on ropes, prying with timbers, stanchions, crowbars, and whatever else they could find, dragged the corpse to the edge of the

Jumbo dies so that Tom Thumb may live in these fanciful views of the elephant's last minutes. According to Barnum, Jumbo hurled his small friend to safety and charged the oncoming locomotive. The true story is less romantic but no less spectacular.

embankment and rolled it over.

As the large crowd milled around, souvenir hunters, armed with knives and scissors, moved in immediately on the body, though circus men protected it as well as they could. Scott, numbed with shock, grief, and exhaustion, lay down on his old friend's remains and went to sleep so soundly that he was not awakened by one particularly audacious souvenir hunter who removed a large slice from one of Jumbo's ears. When he later discovered the mutilation, he became nearly hysterical. The next morning, however, the St. Thomas police arrived and kept a twenty-four-hour guard to prevent further vandalism.

Barnum was at the Murray Hill Hotel when he was first told of the disaster in St. Thomas. The reporters gathered around his breakfast table, and the old showman stated mournfully, "The loss is tremendous," then recovered himself to continue piously, "but such a trifle never disturbs my nerves. Have I not lost a million dollars by fires, and half as much by other financial misfortunes?"

The financial loss was considerable, including not only the $150,000 at which Jumbo was valued but also the huge gate receipts produced by the elephant. Barnum did not carry insurance for anything like that amount. He did sue the Grand Trunk for a hundred thousand dollars, but more for the publicity value than in any real expectation of recovery; and he settled out of court for a relative pittance.

Yet Barnum's stoicism before the press was not entirely feigned. He was not prepared to let death cheat him of the money that would have been paid by future visitors to the elephant. He would have Jumbo stuffed and continue to exhibit him, in his "museum." He gave the impression that this was a brilliant spur-of-the-moment counter to fate, but actually

Barnum had long since arranged to have Jumbo's hide and skeleton mounted in the event of some mishap. In 1883 he had written to Professor Henry A. Ward, the manager of a firm dealing in commercially prepared natural science exhibits for museums:

Dear Sir:
On my return home I found your letter of August 29. I shall have my managers understand that if we lose Jumbo (which Heaven forbid) you must be telegraphed immediately, and I hope you will lose no time in saving his skin and skeleton. As to the other animals, I will talk with you about them at the close of the season—a fortnight hence.

Truly yours,
P. T. Barnum

Though Ward was telegraphed immediately after Jumbo's demise, it was the seventeenth before he arrived on the scene with his assistants, W. J. Crutchley and nineteen-year-old Carl E. Akeley. The latter was a teenage genius who later gave taxidermy a high degree of artistic realism and created the celebrated Akeley Hall in the American Museum of Natural History in New York. Jumbo had been lying dead for nearly two days, guarded constantly from the mobs of souvenir hunters. By the time Ward had measured every dimension of the body and raided all the neighboring towns in a quest for a half dozen butchers to begin the dissection, the odors wafting through the railyard had become distracting. The dissection lasted all afternoon and evening, and much of it had to be done from the inside, a morbid task that fell to a Mr. Peters, who later commented that he knew what Jonah must have gone through inside the big fish. Afterward the meat and scraps were cremated on a great pyre of four cords of wood.

The sections of the 1,538-pound hide were at once put in baths of salt water and alum and shipped to Rochester in a wooden tank. Back at Ward's establishment, where a special building had to be erected to

provide enough room, Akeley was deputed to figure out how to mount an elephant skin sturdily enough to stand rail travel, as Barnum insisted it must do.

Akeley set to work; the skin was cured, scraped, and treated with arsenic to eliminate the danger of decay. A wooden manikin was built to his careful specifications, made from measurements of the actual corpse. When it was ready, the skin was stretched over the form and fastened down with forty-four thousand countersunk copper nails.

The 2,400-pound skeleton was packed in boxes and shipped back to the establishment, where a special brick tank had to be built to macerate the bones. The greatest problem was the splintered skull. Akeley managed to reassemble its shards with papier-mâché on a special wooden framework that he designed. He did it so well that to the present time the cracks are practically invisible.

Barnum had specified that the mountings, suitable for rugged rail travel, were to be ready by March of 1886. When Akeley finished his monumental work, special wagons were designed, and the two Jumbos—bones and hide—were signed over to Barnum's men on March 4, 1886. The unveiling of the specimens had already taken place on February 26 at Rochester's Powers Hotel, at a lavish banquet during which Barnum served reporters a jelly made out of part of Jumbo's powdered tusks.

Meanwhile, the redoubtable old showman was building a fevered interest among his public to see the remains of the immortal Jumbo. The first step was to publish his own account of Jumbo's violent end, a wild bit of inspired invention. The noble Jumbo, Barnum maintained, had sacrificed his own life in a valiant attempt to save the life of the little clown elephant, Tom Thumb. Jumbo had "snatched the little elephant from in front of the thundering train and hurled the little fellow twenty yards to safety." With Tom Thumb safe, continued the master publicist, Jumbo turned to face the oncoming freight. "The leviathan of the rail and the mountain of bone and brawn came together with a crash that made the solid roadbed quake. . . . Jumbo . . . gave but one groan after being struck and then assumed an attitude of determination and composed himself to meet death with a becoming dignity and fortitude."

The second step in his post-mortem Jumbo campaign was the acquisition of the placid Alice, the stolid old cow elephant of the London Zoo. She was imported as Jumbo's weeping widow, though in fact Alice had never shown any interest in Jumbo and they were both too young to mate for much of the time they were together. The third step was to train all the other elephants in the circus to wipe their eyes with black-bordered sheets.

For the next two seasons Jumbo's skin and skeleton led the grand parade, riding in a specially designed wagon and followed by the "widowed" Alice and her entire herd of attendants, all holding those black-trimmed sheets in their trunks and wiping their eyes. The scheme was wildly successful as an audience attraction. But then, in the winter of 1887–88, the circus winter headquarters at Bridgeport, Connecticut, burned to the ground. Poor Alice perished in the flames, although Jumbo's precious remains were saved.

By then, however, Barnum was ready to drop the Jumbo theme from his Greatest Show on Earth. In a typical gesture he donated the great skeleton to the American Museum of Natural History in New York and the stuffed skin to Tufts University near Boston, of which he was a founder and trustee. Only Barnum, notes one writer, would have figured out a way to exhibit his prime attraction in two

places at the same time, two hundred miles apart.

The morose little Matthew Scott followed Jumbo to Tufts. Unable to accept the fact that the elephant was really dead, he became pathetically dotty. Often he was seen sitting by the gigantic stuffed figure, dusting it and talking to it. Later, it appears from available evidence, he returned penniless to England and dropped out of sight.

After two years Barnum recalled his bequests from retirement long enough for two tours of Europe, then returned them to the original beneficiaries, where they have remained ever since. Today the skeleton presides peacefully over the Synoptic Hall of the American Museum of Natural History. The skin, towering within the Barnum Museum of Tufts University, now serves as the mascot of that school, where for many years tradition had it that coins dropped in the trunk brought "A's" on exams.

The skeleton in New York stands a trifle less than eleven feet two inches tall at the shoulder, which gives some indication of the animal's actual height, probably close to eleven feet seven inches. But the skin is another matter entirely. Barnum's instruc-

This article is James L. Haley's first published work. A senior at the University of Texas at Arlington, he is currently doing research for a book on the Red River War of 1874–5.

tions concerning the mounting were "By all means let [the skin] show as large as possible. It will be a grand thing to take all advantage possible in this direction. Let him show like a mountain." He got his way, as Akeley obliged him and stretched the skin upward to a larger-than-life twelve feet even. And to complete the reconstruction the tusks, which had been shattered in the accident, were replaced by genuine ivory substitutes.

It was a fitting end to Jumbo's dazzling career, throughout which it was Barnum's stated intention to see all the dry little words like "huge," "mammoth," and "colossal" stricken from the dictionary, to be replaced by one all-new, all-purpose, all-encompassing adjective: "jumbo." He did not completely succeed, but any exposure to the language of ballyhoo even today shows that the champion of humbug came remarkably close.

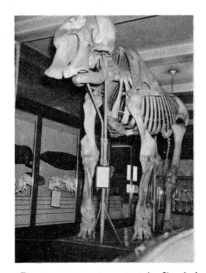 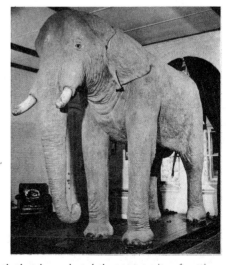

Barnum was not so upset by Jumbo's death that he neglected the opportunity of getting two elephants for the price of one. He displayed both bones and skin for a while, then donated the former to the American Museum of Natural History and the latter to Tufts.

The General of General Motors
CONTINUED FROM PAGE 16

For a time Durant had a bedroom at the home of his daughter and her husband, Dr. Edwin Campbell, a Flint physician she married in April, 1906. Margery's privately printed 1929 biography, *My Father*, has been appropriately described as "a work of filial piety." In it Margery remembered her father as "a very clean man: an immaculate man." Still, he "smoked cigars almost incessantly—I almost never saw him without one." Durant ate very little, hurriedly and mechanically. He "slept only two or three hours a night." He disliked outdoor exercise, open windows, and cold weather. He was always too busy to buy new clothes, so he generally ordered his suits on approval by phone. "He always had a bag packed ready to go." And it seemed to Margery that "he spent most of his life travelling.... He never planned ahead; he just went." She found him an affectionate and considerate father, even though "he doesn't ever give all of his inner self to those about him."

The most significant omission in Margery's book is that she makes no mention of Durant's taking, in 1908, a second wife, Catherine Lederer of Jackson, Michigan, the bright and pretty teen-age daughter of a railroad employee. Durant was forty-seven at the time, Catherine younger than Margery. It is a good guess that Margery jealously felt displaced by her father's charming young wife.

Despite the age difference, or maybe in part because of it, Durant found an ideal mate in Catherine. Her devotion to him was constant through a hectic career that involved as many failures as successes. The marriage was childless but otherwise idyllic. Catherine never had to fear that Durant's affections would stray: his life was amazingly free from any breath of scandal. That he practiced a strait-laced morality was learned the hard way by a Los Angeles Durant Motors dealer who gave a party to honor the founder's visit to southern California. When Durant entered the railroad car that had been rented for the occasion and saw that liquor and women were prominently aboard, he muttered a few caustic remarks and left. The dealer's franchise was cancelled. Durant's main diversion when travelling was playing checkers on the small checkerboard he carried around in his pocket.

By the time he married Catherine, Durant had built Buick into the leading automobile producer in the United States. In 1908 the company built 8,487 cars, had a net worth of $3.5 million, and occupied the largest automobile plant in the world. Nevertheless Durant was worried about the immediate future. So was Benjamin Briscoe, president of the Maxwell-Briscoe Motor Company, one of Buick's chief competitors.

Whereas Henry Ford was confident by 1908 that his Model T was the "car for the great multitude," Billy Durant was more uncertain than ever about the best bet in automotive technology. So he decided to play the field. His rationale was revealed in a later lament, "They say I shouldn't have bought Cartercar. Well, how was anyone to know that Cartercar wasn't to be the thing? It had the friction drive and no other car had it. ... And then there's Elmore with its two-cycle engine ... maybe a two-cycle motor was going to be the thing.... I was for getting every kind of thing in sight, playing it safe all along the line."

Benjamin Briscoe also found conditions in the spring of 1908 "somewhat ominous, especially for such concerns as had large fixed investments in plants, machinery, tools, etc." Briscoe was worried about "concerns which did not have a worthy car or any manufacturing ability, but with large stock issues to sell, and by ingenious exploitation would succeed in stirring up the trade and the public. ... " He was afraid such companies would force "even the sanest among the manufacturers ... into business risks which they would not have entered had they not been fearful that some other concern would gain a few points on them."

Briscoe and Durant conceived that the answer to these problems was a horizontal and vertical trust. They decided to try "to form a combination of the principal concerns in the industry ... for the purpose of having one big concern of such dominating influence in the automobile industry, as for instance, the United States Steel Corporation exercises in the steel industry." The easiest way to accomplish this was to merge their own firms, Buick and Maxwell-Briscoe, with several other leading producers of gasoline automobiles. But the merger plan failed when Henry Ford and Ransom E. Olds each demanded three million dollars in cash to sell out, instead of the securities Briscoe and Durant offered.

Undaunted, Briscoe and Durant hatched another consolidation scheme. They secured a New Jersey charter for an International Motors Company, with J. P. Morgan & Company to underwrite the stock issue. This plan fell through, too, when the House of Morgan withdrew its support. During the negotiations Durant correctly prophesied that soon a half million automobiles would be sold annually in the United States. George W. Perkins, who represented the Morgan interests, curtly suggested that when Durant wanted to borrow money, he had better keep such crazy notions to himself. By this time Briscoe had had enough. He and Durant parted company.

Working alone now, Durant moved quickly to form the General Motors Company as a New Jersey holding company with a nominal capitalization of only two thousand dollars on September 16, 1908. The holding-company structure allowed Durant, who was short of both cash and bank credit, to finance his combination mainly through exchange of stock. Cadillac, purchased for a premium $4.5 million, was the most notable of the few companies for which cash had to be paid. General Motors soon acquired control of thirteen motor-vehicle and ten parts-and-accessories manufacturers that varied considerably in strength, prominence, and potential. Its capitalization reached an astonishing sixty million dollars within a year.

But General Motors was in trouble from the start. Durant's attempt at "getting every thing in sight, playing it safe all along the line" turned out to be catastrophic. He bought too many weak units that drained off the profits from a few strong companies. The most spectacular error was purchasing the Heany Lamp Company for seven million dollars in General Motors stock to obtain a patent on an incandescent lamp that turned out to be fraudulent. Only two of the thirteen automobile manufacturers in the combination he threw together, Buick and Cadillac, were making money. And as Durant dispersed his energies Buick began to decline, threatening to leave Cadillac alone among the automobile-manufacturing units to support the heavily overcapitalized holding company. Durant was so optimistic about demand that he failed to build up cash reserves, to get adequate information about the combination's financial condition, and to achieve economies through coordinating and integrating the constituent units of General Motors.

The crunch came when sales unexpectedly dropped as a result of a slight business recession in 1910. Durant was unable to meet his payroll and bills from suppliers. The First National Bank of Boston, to whom Buick was indebted for seven million dollars, called in a banking syndicate that agreed to save the General Motors combination—but only after receiving assurances of feasibility and support from Henry M. Leland and Wilfred C. Leland of Cadillac and extracting stiff concessions. They received over six million dollars in General Motors stock plus fifteen million in five-year, 6 per cent notes for a $12.75-million cash loan. Durant was to remain as vice president and a member of the board of directors of General Motors. But he was forced to retire from active management, and the banking syndicate gained control of the combination through a five-year voting trust. Durant's power as one of the trustees was negated by the other four, who represented the bankers.

To the leadership of General Motors the bankers appointed James J. Storrow, a senior partner in the Boston house of Lee, Higginson, who served first as the temporary president and then directed operations as chairman of the finance committee. Charles W. Nash, who had succeeded Durant as head of Buick in 1910, was moved to the presidency in 1912. Walter P. Chrysler, manager of the American Locomotive Works, was then brought in to take over Nash's position at Buick.

The Storrow-Nash regime followed a conservative policy of retrenchment during their five-year period of control. Only five companies were allowed to continue to manufacture motor vehicles—Buick, Cadillac, General Motors Truck, Oakland, and Oldsmobile. A centralized research and testing program was initiated, and internal administration was improved. But they made the crucial error of withholding common-stock dividends. This increased the propensity of General Motors stockholders to sell their shares to Durant, who, down but by no means out, was anxious to regain control of the combination.

Within a year after the bankers took control of General Motors, Durant started his comeback. While still a substantial stockholder in General Motors, in 1911 he formed two new companies to manufacture automobiles: the Little Motor Company in Flint, to build a small, four-cylinder runabout that sold for only $650, and the Chevrolet Motor Car Company in Detroit, to build a light, moderately priced car designed by Louis Chevrolet, a Swiss mechanic who had been one of Buick's racing drivers. After forming and folding two other companies, Durant then abandoned Little and concentrated his energies on Chevrolet. The Chevrolet manufacturing operations were transferred to Flint—and Louis Chevrolet was arbitrarily fired the third time he walked into Durant's office with a cigarette dangling from his lips. Durant had abruptly quit smoking and could no longer tolerate the habit in anyone else.

Nearly sixteen thousand cars that bore Chevrolet's name were sold in the two years ending August 14, 1915. Durant announced that he would bring out a new $490 model to compete with the Ford Model T; and in September, 1915, he organized the Chevrolet Motor Company of Delaware as a holding company for all Chevrolet activities. Raising its capitalization to eighty million dollars, all common stock, Durant offered to trade five shares of Chevrolet for one share of General Motors. There were so many takers that the offer was closed on January 26, 1916.

Durant's return to control was imminent by the time the General Motors voting trust expired on October 1, 1915. Early that year Durant and Pierre S. du Pont began buying up General Motors stock in the open market with the aid of Louis G. Kaufman, president of the Chatham and Phoenix Bank of New York City. Du Pont and John J. Raskob, treasurer of E. I. du Pont de Nemours and Company, saw General Motors as an ideal place to reinvest their huge profits from World War 1 munitions sales. Some twenty-seven million dollars of du Pont's money helped push General Motors common stock from a quotation of 82 on January 2, 1915, to a high for the year of 558.

It was summer before the banker-dominated management at General Motors realized what was happening.

At a meeting of the General Motors directors and large stockholders on September 16, 1915, Kaufman and du Pont were elected to the board of directors, du Pont as its chairman. A belated attempt by Durant's opponents to mobilize stockholder support for another three-year voting trust failed. With the votes of about 40 per cent of the General Motors common stock in his pocket, Durant proceeded to announce calmly: "Gentlemen, I now control this company."

With the resignation of Charles W. Nash on June 1, 1916, Durant regained the presidency of General Motors. He took over a much stronger combination than he had left five years before. The du Pont alliance eased the problem of obtaining working capital. Chevrolet was a moneymaking addition to the General Motors manufacturing units. Strength was also added by the acquisition of the United Motors Corporation, a Durant-created holding company owning the securities of five leading automobile-accessory manufacturers. With United Motors came Charles F. Kettering, the engineering genius, and Alfred P. Sloan, Jr. Recognizing the need to integrate and consolidate his impressive new empire, Durant reincorporated the General Motors Company, a New Jersey holding company, as the General Motors Corporation of Delaware, an operating company, on October 13, 1916.

Some of Durant's new moves turned out to be brilliant. The Fisher Body Company was purchased in 1918. And recognizing well ahead of his contemporaries that the automobile industry could not continue on a cash-on-delivery basis, Durant pioneered in time sales for expensive consumer goods with the creation of the General Motors Acceptance Corporation in 1919. Against everyone's advice he paid fifty-six thousand dollars for a faltering, one-man electric-refrigerator company that served only forty-two customers, on the ground that refrigerators were related to automobiles—both were essentially cases containing motors. A contest to find a name for the company was won by "Frigidaire."

The trouble was that Durant lacked the judgment to discriminate among the many ideas about which he became enthusiastic. For every Buick there was a Cartercar; for every Frigidaire there was a Heany Lamp. Durant's idea of "playing it safe all along the line," backing every impulse in the hope that some would pan out, made him an inveterate expansionist who could survive only in flush times. His performance was brilliant when he concentrated his considerable energies upon building up a single company in an expanding market, as at Durant-Dort, Buick, and Chevrolet. But his bent toward indiscriminate dispersal of his energies and one-man rule spelled disaster

when times got tight and the profits from a few phenomenally successful bets began to dwindle. Sorry examples were two new passenger cars that Durant added to the General Motors line for no apparent reason: the Sheridan and the Scripps-Booth. Both were losers. But even had they proved popular, they would merely have competed in the same general price range with Buick, Chevrolet, Oakland, and Oldsmobile. As in 1910, by 1921 only Buick and Cadillac were making money for General Motors.

The enthusiasm that Durant developed to get into the farm-machinery business was more understandable. Impressed by the initial success of the Fordson tractor, Durant developed an obsession to "lick Henry Ford in the manufacture of tractors" and, while he was at it, to "lick the International Harvester Company in the manufacture of agricultural implements."

In 1917 Durant bought into the Samson Sieve-Grip Tractor Company, of Stockton, California, manufacturers of a tractor called the Iron Horse, which was guided by reins. He later added two other small agricultural-machine companies and formed the Samson Tractor Division of General Motors. In addition to the Iron Horse, a lighter "Samson" tractor was developed to compete with the Fordson. Plans for a nine-passenger farmer's car that would sell for only seven hundred dollars never materialized because it became obvious there was no way to build it at a profit. The Samson tractor and the Iron Horse were returned in droves by irate farmers who demanded their money back. The tractor-division fiasco cost General Motors a sum variously estimated as between thirteen and forty-two million dollars before it was liquidated in 1920.

Relationships with key associates were severed as Durant became more and more difficult to work with. Charles W. Nash was the first to go. Next, Henry M. Leland and Wilfred C. Leland left Cadillac to form Lincoln in 1917 over the refusal of Durant, a pacifist by inclination, to endorse their enthusiasm for the war effort. Other executives grew frustrated by Durant's chaotic schedule, inability to recognize priorities, and increasingly heavy involvement in the stock market. Walter P. Chrysler was called to New York by Durant. "For several days in succession," he said later, "I waited at his office, but he was so busy he could not take the time to talk with me. It seemed to me he was trying to keep in communication with half the continent; eight or ten telephones were lined up on his desk. . . . 'Durant is buying' was a potent phrase in Wall Street then." Alfred P. Sloan, Jr., also recalled that executives lounged around the room watching Durant's barber, Jake, shave him "while our scheduled work was neglected." At executive meetings "the ten or fifteen of us who gathered there would wait all day for the Chief . . . old friends could not easily be denied, and so we had to wait."

As the stock market came to absorb his attention Durant relied on cronies and made important decisions off the top of his head. Sloan was aghast that a car model was tested on a supposed cross-country trip by the same man who designed it; he dispatched reports, enthusiastically received by Durant, "by conniving with hotel porters along his scheduled route" while never actually making the trip. Sloan was even more aghast at Durant's casual attitude about the location and price of the new General Motors Building in Detroit, a twenty-million-dollar project that Durant later opposed as too costly. "He started at the corner of Cass Avenue, paced a certain distance west on West Grand Boulevard past the old Hyatt Building. . . . Then he stopped, for no apparent reason, at some apartment houses on the other side of the building. He said that this was about all the ground we wanted, and turned to me and said, as well as I can remember, 'Alfred, will you go and buy these properties for us and Mr. Prentis will pay whatever you decide to pay for them.'"

By 1919 Walter P. Chrysler was worried that "Buick was making about half the money [earned by General Motors], but the corporation was spending much faster than we could earn." Insult was added to injury when Durant sold the lucrative Detroit Buick branch house to a crony without consulting Chrysler. The end came when Durant promised the city of Flint a six-million-dollar frame plant. Chrysler was convinced that Flint lacked adequate facilities, and knew that the plant would "cost more in five years than we would pay for frames in ten." Though Durant later backed down, Chrysler soon left, saying to Sloan, who tried to talk him into staying: "No, I'm washed up. I just can't stand the way the thing is being run. All I'm anxious about now is to sell my stock."

Sloan was soon on the verge of resigning himself. He could no longer tolerate the one-man rule of an inveterate gambler who ignored facts to make decisions on the basis of "some intuitive flash of brilliance." His ideal executive was the security-oriented technician who, sensitive to the opinions of others, worked well as a member of an entrepreneurial team. Sloan took a vacation abroad to think things over early in the summer of 1920. When he returned in August, he "sensed something unusual" and decided "I'll ride along awhile and see what happens." What Sloan "sensed" was that Durant's days at General Motors were numbered.

Almost sixty, Durant did not recognize adequately that the business environment was changing rapidly in the automobile industry. An incurable optimist, he was also banking on an uninterrupted post-World War I boom in automobile sales. He was unprepared, as were Henry Ford and many others, for the sharp recession that accompanied conversion to a peacetime economy. General Motors was caught in the midst of an expansion program that could not have been more ill-timed. The working capital of the corporation had been dissipated. So an issue of sixty-four million dollars in common stock was offered for underwriting. Thirty-six million of the issue was picked up by an English-Canadian banking syndicate at twenty dollars a share, but that still left twenty-eight million dollars to be disposed of in a declining market. And the crisis deepened as the stock issue quickly became essential to the survival of General Motors.

The expansion program, initiated in 1918, was not Durant's error alone. By 1919 the du Pont interests owned 28.7 per cent of the General Motors common stock, and Pierre S. du Pont, chairman of the corporation's board of directors, had supported the expansion without objection. John J. Raskob, the du Pont treasurer, who was chairman of the General Motors finance committee, was at least as responsible as Durant for enthusiastically promoting the program. But wherever the fault lay, other large General Motors stockholders, concerned about what was happening, began to unload their holdings. Durant saw that this could collapse the price of General Motors stock, with the disastrous result that it might be impossible to dispose of the remaining twenty-eight million dollars of the new issue. He also wanted to protect the value of his personal holdings, which on paper were worth $105 million. But despite Durant's attempt to snap up large blocks as they were offered for sale, the stock slid from $38.50 to under thirty dollars a share before a syndicate headed by J. P. Morgan & Company agreed to underwrite the remaining twenty-eight million of the new issue.

On July 15, 1920, the Morgan interests announced that the twenty-eight million dollars in stock had been disposed of. But Durant's troubles were just beginning. There was either a misunderstanding or a conflict with the House of Morgan and its financial allies. In either case the Morgan men dumped a hundred thousand shares of General Motors stock on the market, driving the price down to $20.50. As the stock continued to tumble, Durant bought frantically in a desperate attempt to salvage something. Operating heavily on margin, he supported the stock down to twelve dollars a share before he admitted he was licked. Durant's cash resources were wiped out, and he owed over twenty million dollars to twenty-one brokers and three banks.

The du Ponts, Raskob, and the House of Morgan became afraid that if Durant declared bankruptcy, he might drag down with him the brokers, banks, and General Motors. At a series of meetings in November, 1920, they worked out an alternative. They would bail Durant out of the mess on the condition that he hand over to them control of General Motors. Durant came out of the deal with about three million dollars of General Motors stock plus a personal loan of five hundred thousand from Pierre S. du Pont.

Durant resigned as president on November 30, 1920. "You knew he was grief-stricken, but no grief showed in his face. He was smiling pleasantly, as if it were a routine matter, when he told us he was resigning," remembered Sloan. The following day Durant cleaned out his desk. When he was leaving the building, he turned to remark: "Well, May first is usually the national moving day, but we seem to have changed it into December first."

To allay fears in Flint about Durant's resignation and the "take-over" of General Motors by eastern bankers, the new management built a three-hundred-thousand-dollar hotel in Flint and named it the Hotel Durant—the impersonal corporation's final tribute to a founder who had outlived his usefulness to the firm.

The Durant name still had magic. The Goodrich Tire & Rubber Company invited Durant to set himself up in a modest office in its building in New York City. After a brief holiday at White Sulphur Springs Durant contacted sixty-seven friends, asking them to back a new automobile company that would bear his name. Within forty-eight hours he raised seven million dollars, two million more than he needed. Durant Motors, Inc., came into being on January 21, 1921.

The enterprise started under propitious conditions. Durant's public image was excellent. He was looked upon as an underdog, a self-made man who had been crucified by the du Ponts and the Wall Street bankers. The first model produced, the "Durant four," was an exceptional value at $850; as Durant advertised it, it was "a real good car."

Durant Motors, Inc., grew by leaps and bounds. Facilities were built in Flint and Lansing and in Oakland, California. The Sheridan plant in Muncie, Indiana, was bought to produce the "Durant six." The bankrupt Locomobile Company of Bridgeport, Connecticut, was purchased to add to the Durant line a luxury car with a long-standing, prestigious reputation. With the Willys Corporation in receivership, Chrysler and Studebaker were outbid at $5.25 million to acquire the new Willys plant at Elizabeth, New Jersey, the most modern automobile factory in the world, plus the Willys design for a medium-priced car that became the "Flint." Then, on February 15, 1922, Durant announced that he would bring out the "Star," which at a price of $348 would compete with the Ford Model T. Cognizant of Ford's patent anti-Semitism, Durant thought the Star would have a special appeal to Jewish buyers. Some sixty thousand people flocked to see the Star at its first showing in New York City, and by January 1, 1923, Durant had accepted cash deposits on orders for 231,000 Stars, a full year's production. The Durant Motors Acceptance Corporation was formed to finance time sales and to help dealers store cars over the winter for spring delivery. Ever a financial innovator, Durant worked out an ingenious scheme for financing his new company by selling stock at low prices, on the installment plan. He got 146,000 shareholders—more than any other American company except American Telephone and Telegraph. And he created the Liberty National Bank, to raise still more money. He called it "the most democratic bank in the United States." Its officers and board of directors worked without salary. Anyone could purchase stock in it. No one was allowed to own more than one of its three hundred thousand shares, which could be purchased on the installment plan.

Yet despite its promising start, Durant Motors never amounted to much. In its best years it was unable to capture more than a fifth of the market for new cars. Henry Ford effectively crushed the threat of competition from the Star by unexpectedly lowering his prices for the Model T. Other Durant models never caught the fancy of the buying public. And anyway, by the mid-1920's the market for new cars was rapidly approaching the saturation point.

A well-managed firm might have pulled through—but Durant failed to recruit top-flight managerial talent. Few of his more capable associates at General Motors had left with him. They knew that with Durant business was a roller-coaster ride that was apt to end in a crash. And in the automobile industry the word had gotten around that Durant was difficult to work for. That put the burden of managing Durant Motors squarely on Durant's shoulders. He might have succeeded if he had applied his energies fully to the task. But he could not resist the lure of the stock market, and soon he started to treat Durant Motors as a sideline.

After the First World War the dominant power that the eastern investment bankers historically had wielded in Wall Street increasingly came to be shared with a new group of self-made millionaires who came mainly from the Midwest. Less cautious and conservative than their predecessors, these new speculators became the prime movers in the runaway bull market of the late 1920's. The most important figure among them by far was William C. Durant, who after 1924 was widely referred to by the press as "the leading bull."

The "bull consortium" that Durant led was estimated at various times to include between twenty and thirty millionaire investors, who were known as Durant's prosperity boys. It was said that Durant himself had $1.2 billion in the market by 1928 and that he directly controlled about four billion in investments. Durant had accounts with at least fifteen brokers, and his commission fees to brokers were rumored to run as high as six million dollars a year. Phone bills of twenty thousand dollars a week were supposedly not uncommon. The financial press regularly reported multimillion-dollar killings that Durant was said to have made in individual pools.

Durant, like many other insiders, unloaded in the spring of 1929. Shortly after the collapse of the market on Tuesday, October 29, Earl Sparling, a financial writer, visited Durant to get his comment on the fact that some forty billion dollars in security values had been wiped out overnight. Durant did some quick calculations on a pad of paper, smiled, and announced that if the loss were translated into a stack of silver dollars, it would reach a hundred thousand miles into the sky.

But like many others who had sold before the initial disaster struck, Durant assumed that the worst was now over. He plunged back into the market to pick up stocks at what he thought were bargain prices, only to find that the market kept deteriorating. His brokers sold him out in 1930.

Durant scraped together his remaining resources and plowed them into Durant Motors. Conceiving that the American market was ripe for a small car with low initial and maintenance costs, he started to manufacture the French "Mathis" in New Jersey. Ultimately the Volkswagen was to prove him right, but at the outset of the Great Depression not even Billy Durant could revitalize the corpse that Durant Motors had become.

Durant Motors was liquidated in 1933. Bankruptcy for Durant followed in 1936, when he declared liabilities of almost one million dollars versus assets of only $250 (his clothes). Raymere, the elegant home at Deal, was sold complete with furnishings at auction in 1938 and brought $111,778. Through it all Durant managed to hang onto his apartments in New York City and at the Hotel Durant in Flint, and enough money to provide him and Catherine with a comfortable living for their remaining years.

A short time after the bankruptcy proceedings reporters acting on an anonymous tip found William Crapo Durant washing dishes in a five-cent hamburger joint attached to a supermarket that had recently opened in an old Durant Motors salesroom at Asbury Park, New Jersey. Looking at least two decades younger than his seventy-five years, Billy obligingly posed with a broom, sweeping out the supermarket, too. It was a publicity stunt. Durant owned both the supermarket and the lunch counter. His nephew confided to the reporters: "Mr. Durant is just as enthusiastic over building up the Food Market as he ever was over automobiles. In fact he no longer can bear the thought of an automobile." Supermarkets would be a big thing one day. But not then. Durant lost the place in a few months' time.

Nineteen forty found Durant trying to start a chain of bowling alleys in the Midwest. He had conceived that recreation was the industry of the future and that a bowling alley serving only nonalcoholic beverages would appeal to young people and families. Opening his first bowling alley in his hometown of Flint, he tried to be helpful and to make friends of all the bowlers. The idea was excellent, but Durant again was ahead of his time.

Durant's health failed, and for most of his remaining years he was an invalid. But his interest in taking another flier never failed. Looking forward to the post-World War II boom, in late 1943 Durant wrote to W. H. Washer, a Flint inventor: "When you have developed anything novel that appeals to you, don't be afraid to give 'Uncle Bill' an opportunity of joining the workers' ranks." At the war's end Durant told the Flint *Journal,* in a formal statement through his secretary: "The consumer market needs everything at home and abroad. The demand is so great there virtually is no competition and no sales resistance." He predicted a three- to seven-year boom. Reminiscent of his early days hawking patent medicine, yet foreshadowing the sixties, when the cosmetics industry would come into its own, Durant's last business venture was backing a nostrum to prevent baldness and cure dandruff.

Billy Durant once said: "Money? What is money? It is only loaned to a man; he comes into the world with nothing and he leaves with nothing." It was a characteristic statement, and a suitable epitaph.

James J. Flink teaches comparative culture at the University of California, Irvine; he is the author of America Adopts the Automobile, 1895-1910 *(M.I.T. Press, 1970). Glenn A. Niemeyer is dean of the College of Arts and Sciences at Grand Valley State College, Allendale, Michigan, and is the author of* The Automotive Career of Ransom E. Olds *(Michigan State University Press, 1963). Together they are working on a full-length biography of Durant.*

Historian by Serendipity

CONTINUED FROM PAGE 32

ing to an Ogden librarian, Madeline McQuown, DeVoto said:

Very few historians of our time, practically no academic historians, realize that history is not only knowledge, not only knowledge and wisdom even, but is also an art. I do. My books employ the methods and techniques of literature and especially they have structure as literature. They have form.... Form is used to reveal meaning.... You are quite right in perceiving that the books are like novels—they are constructed and written like novels, to exactly the same end as novels.... Finally, the materials of history have become so multifarious that, I think, from now on some kinds of history can be written satisfactorily only by methods which I have used ... and may possibly be the first to have used ... methods which I can designate roughly as the test-boring and the focus on simultaneousness.

These techniques are worth a glance. What he calls the "test-boring" is what Robert Frost meant when he called himself a Synecdochist. "All that an artist needs is samples," Frost said. The part might represent the whole, one illustration might prove more than a whole catalogue. In that spirit DeVoto let the year 1846 encapsulate the whole history of the frontier. His "narrative history of a year" did not prove his thesis, it illustrated it as possibility; and his sampling permitted the re-creation of brilliant historical scenes and minimized dull chronological connective tissue. By one form of test-boring, certain individuals—in this book the mountain man Jim Clyman—became true "culture heroes," archetypes. When DeVoto had stumbled upon Clyman, away back in 1933, he had known instantly what use he would make of him.

Simultaneity, too, was a device he had used in *Mark Twain's America* and would use again in *Across the Wide Missouri*. "A chronological symphony," Frederic Paxson called it; it was familiar enough in the impressionistic novel but strange to history, and sometimes bewildering, for it meant moving many stories forward by small increments. At Henry Canby's request DeVoto rewrote the first chaper of *The Year of Decision: 1846*, tempering his wind to the Book-of-the-Month Club's lambs, but even rewritten it was complex and difficult until the reader adjusted himself to the method. A decade after he finished *The Year of Decision: 1846*, DeVoto told his friend and physician Herbert Scheinberg, "I wrote the book deliberately with the technique you will soon perceive. The technique forfeits nine out of ten readers. My theory is, however, that the tenth will get much more out of it than if I had used a different and easier technique. I was trying to suggest, as well as prose enables a writer to suggest, that all these actions were occurring at the same time." He was also trying to enlist his readers as collaborators. "In narrative, fewest is best," he advised Mattingly. "If a reader

is with you at all, he's half a yard ahead of you."

Vivid scenes, novelistic characters, selected incidents, symbolic culture heroes, the abiding presence of a judging intelligence, impressionistic brevity, these are the elements of the kind of history natural to a novelist. He accepted the obligation to be accurate, and he followed such preceptors as Schlesinger in his concentration on social history; but from there on he went his own way, and his way assumed that there "is no boundary between history and literature; each holds a large part of its field in common with the other."

Test-boring and simultaneity had given DeVoto the form and focus for *The Year of Decision*. They would operate in his next history as well, but serendipity would find the subject of *Across the Wide Missouri* for him. In April, 1944, following his formula of going to an expert and being helpless, he asked Henry Steele Commager for advice on how and where to learn the backgrounds of the Louisiana Purchase and other matters. He was going to write a narrative history of the Lewis and Clark expedition. But something else had already interrupted that project before he ever wrote Commager. In February a Hungarian émigré named Emery Reves had brought into the Houghton Mifflin office a hundred or more water colors and sketches painted in the West in 1837, when the artist, Alfred Jacob Miller of Baltimore, was employed by a Scottish baronet, Sir William Drummond Stewart, who wanted hunting pictures for his castle. The pictures now belonged to Mrs. Clyde Porter of Missouri. Reves was going to publish them and wanted a competent western historian to write twenty thousand words of captions. Dixon Wecter had suggested DeVoto.

DeVoto looked over the drawings and knew them at once to be a priceless historical find, a gallery of the mountain fur trade in its climactic year. He would be happy to do the captions, though he thought twenty thousand words not enough. Thus lightly, the way he might have agreed to write a magazine article, he set out into the fur trade. But the negotiations were sticky: Reves' part in the transaction was obscure and had to be defined, Mrs. Porter's biographical essay on Stewart had to be all but discarded as incompetent. It was a year before the dickering was done, and by that time the book had altered. The twenty thousand words of captions would be forty thousand, or even more, and the title would not be "The Stewart-Miller Expedition." That expedition, as DeVoto wrote Mrs. Porter, was going to be used "only as a line to hang the whole fur trade on."

By pure accident he had arrived at the book he had been unconsciously preparing himself to write for twenty years. He could finally express at full length, but within the form that suited him best, the enthusiasm he had felt for the mountain men when he was a romantic boy in Ogden Canyon, walking dust that had been printed by the moccasins of heroes. He could describe and celebrate skills he had admired and imitated, and he could tie the fur trade into the grand theme of the westward expansion. Here in these adventurers was Manifest Destiny before it was ever formulated as conscious idea. Here was one of the first and most direct consequences of the expedition of Lewis and Clark, which the Miller pictures had diverted him from. The "little caption job," exciting but casual, which he had thought might take him six weeks, took him three years. A promoter and a woman's-club amateur released him into the large freedom of the mountain past.

God was good to give him Sir William Stewart to hang the whole fur trade on, though it is clear from the way he used Joe Meek and other mountain men that DeVoto could have found unifying culture heroes without Stewart. As in *The Year of Decision: 1846,* recurring and recognized figures braid through the narrative. Encounters in the wilderness suggest remote imperial rivalries. The Oregon question moves up the Columbia and the Snake with Ogden and Ross, the Spanish Southwest comes up from Taos on the Bent's Fort–Fort Laramie trail. Counterespionage or its probability drifts in and out with the enigmatic figure of Captain Benjamin Louis Eulalie de Bonneville, as bald as if scalped and playing the fur trade so improvidently that he *must* have had other motives than profit. Yankee ambition challenges the great fur companies in the person of Nathaniel Wyeth. The partisans whose names are legend lead their brigades through the most romantic wilderness ever known or imagined, performing prodigies of skill, endurance, and war. The Scottish baronet and his party touch here, touch there, live with Indians, hunt buffalo and grizzlies, make the Rendezvous, know familiarly the men in dirty buckskins who are as heroic as anything in Homer and who sit by their fires smelling of bear's grease and singing Injun while their squaws gnaw green hides or pound serviceberries or embroider moccasins with beads and porcupine quills. The artist is there, too, making his quick sketches of things that no pencil or brush has ever recorded or will ever record again with such primal purity.

A romantic wrote *Across the Wide Missouri,* a romantic who knew what he was talking about. DeVoto could not have written as he did about the fur trade, about the dreams that pulled westward men as various as James Dickson and Jed Smith and Henry Spalding, if he had not dreamed those dreams himself and imagined those hardships and practiced those skills and lived in that country. The frontier experience as personal experience, that is his aim. He wants us to be physically disturbed by Narcissa Whitman's most un-Calvinistic charms; he wants us to admire the ingenuity and persistence, even in failure, of

Nat Wyeth; he wants us to recognize in Joe Meek the representative of a savage way of life in transition to something tamer. He wants us to feel the country, the space, the keen air, the color, the danger, of the trapper life.

Something moves in the willows and the Manton is cocked and Sir William stands up in his stirrups—Ephraim is there, Old Caleb, the white bear of the mountains, so terrible that to kill one is a coup as glorious as striking with your bare hand an enemy in his own tipi. For half a mile mules and wagons are stretched out in flat light, dust above the caravan like an opening umbrella, emptiness everywhere, the earth flowing like water at its edges, a false lake hung with groves that have no reality. Here are the braves riding in from the hunt; their faces are like a sorcerer's mask, they are naked to a g-string, the blood of buffalo has soaked their moccasins and dyed their forearms and calves, the squaws wait for them with basins of clear cold water from the Siskadee. . . .

"Sure you're romantic about American history," he wrote Catherine Drinker Bowen when she complained that a professor had put her down. "What your professor left out of account was the fact that it is the most romantic of all histories." That was his mood when he set out to write the Lewis and Clark adventure, and his mood did not change when he got derailed into the fur trade. But when he returned to Lewis and Clark, he found that he could not make it stay a romantic story. It had antecedents and consequences, it spread and spread and spread. To encompass it he had to learn another way of writing history.

In November, 1948, when he had been on *The Course of Empire* about a year, he wrote to Garrett Mattingly, his historical mentor:

On a western expedition in 1837 Alfred Jacob Miller sketched Sir William Drummond Stewart and a buffalo hunter named Antoine.

*W*ho is James K. Polk?'' The Whigs promptly began campaigning on that derision, and there were Democrats who repeated it with a sick concern. The question eventually got an unequivocal answer. Polk had come up the ladder, he was an orthodox party Democrat. He had been Jackson's mouthpiece and floor leader in the House of Representatives, had managed the anti-Bank legislation, had risen to the Speakership, had been governor of Tennessee. But sometimes the belt line shapes an instrument of use and precision. Polk's mind was rigid, narrow, obstinate, far from first-rate. He sincerely believed that only Democrats were truly American, Whigs being either the dupes or the pensioners of England —more, that not only wisdom and patriotism were Democratic monopolies but honor and breeding as well. "Although a Whig he seems a gentleman" is a not uncommon characterization in his diary. He was pompous, suspicious, and secretive; he had no humor; he could be vindictive; and he saw spooks and villains. . . .

But if his mind was narrow it was also powerful and he had guts. If he was orthodox, his integrity was absolute and he could not be scared, manipulated, or brought to heel. No one bluffed him, no one moved him with direct or oblique pressure. Furthermore, he knew how to get things done, which is the first necessity of government, and he knew what he wanted done, which is the second. He came into office with clear ideas and a fixed determination and he was to stand by them through as strenuous an administration as any before Lincoln's. Congress had governed the United States for eight years before him and, after a fashion, was to govern it for the next twelve years after him. But Polk was to govern the United States from 1845 to 1849. He was to be the only "strong" President between Jackson and Lincoln. He was to fix the mold of the future in America down to 1860, and therefore for a long time afterward. That is who James K. Polk was.

Bernard DeVoto, The Year of Decision: 1846

Do I think maybe I'm Francis Parkman? . . . What do you do about geography? I mean, what do I do about it? Have I got to go up the Saskatchewan too? Or Lake Winnipeg? . . . Christ, Mat, I can't dig out the background of the background of the background. . . .

For that matter, why should I? . . . This was supposed to be about Sacajawea, wasn't it? I figure I can clean up the predecessors of L&C in 30 years more, oh, easy. I figure I can do the empires and the wars in less than ten years more and the trans-Allegheny U.S., the state of scientific thought, symmetrical geography, the diplomatics and American politics in another 10, and maybe in 5 years I can get Napoleon and La. straightened out. . . .

Mattingly soothed him with the assurance that he just had a light case of *regressus historicus*. But it was more than a light case. From Lewis and Clark he was led backward to earlier and earlier explorations and at the same time was tempted by what he called in self-derision Historical Ideas, particularly about the ways in which the continent altered the consciousness of its settlers and about the possibility that Jefferson had unadmitted imperialist aims and wanted to take the United States from sea to sea, even before the Louisiana Purchase. Deeper and deeper his research led him. He worried about producing a monstrosity in which "the birth of Christ got a dangling participle and Rome rose and fell in a paragraph." He thought that when he finally began to write, the first word would be "Verrazano," or maybe "Folsom Man."

In the summer of 1950 he had been writing pretty steadily for a year, and everything in his temperament that had been solid was liquid, everything liquid had turned to gas that was escaping at every petcock and threatening to blow the safety valves. Again he took it out on the patient Mattingly:

I have, in nomine Patris et Filii, this day got the French out of North America. One year to the day, and three million words, after I began a book that had no intention of getting the French into North America. . . . So where are we? With thirteen million words written, or by our Lady some two score million, we have now accounted for 229 years that do not enter at all into my book, and have only forty more years to go, or say an even million words, if in the meantime I can learn something about concentration or alternatively get a tight cinch on my bowels, before we reach the beginning of my book and, with a sigh of infinite satisfaction and a suffusing glow of happy realization that only ten million words lie ahead, take up a blank, virgin sheet of paper and write at the top of it Page One.

The fantastic hyperbole reflected the intensity of his effort. He was writing a kind of history, Mattingly told him, quite different from anything he had ever written before, covering centuries instead of focusing a tight dramatic narrative within the span of a year or a handful of years. His tricks of test-boring and simultaneity were of little use; the scope of his subject kept him from developing vivid scenes or extended portraits. At best he could thumbnail and pass on. He felt like the slave of chronology.

"Okay, she's dull," he said resignedly in April, 1951. But even as he said that, he was noting with satisfaction that the book was going to peak right where he had guessed it might, that the English, French, and Spanish explorations in North America came to a confluence on the upper Missouri, from where Lewis and Clark could carry knowledge westward to the sea. He got the Lewis and Clark expedition afloat on the Missouri on page 435 and from there on could write the dramatized and narrative history he liked, the history he had set out to write. But he had created a complex web of context for that adventure; Lewis and Clark were the culmination of what had fascinated him, "the movement of these boys across a map that is not the map they have in their minds." Fable and ignorance were replaced by knowledge in this climactic exploration, and so in the long run, without his conscious manipulation, test-boring worked for DeVoto again.

And it was by no means as dull as he had feared. Mattingly, reading the manuscript in March, 1952, summed it up for him: "And so we come to the Pacific with a sense of having crossed a continent, and a foreknowledge of getting back again, and a premonition of the nation that would cross after us, and the feeling of history shaping us and being shaped by us and emerging from the fluidity of dream or myth into concrete, ineluctable reality. It was an exhilarating experience."

The reviewers found it so. Walter Webb and Henry Nash Smith and Grace Lee Nute applauded it. Henry Commager, who had had a glimpse of it when it was no bigger than a man's hand, thought it "the best book that has been written about the West since Webb's *The Great Plains*, and the best-written book about the West since Parkman." The profession at large, through its representatives, corroborated the reviewers by giving *The Course of Empire* the National Book Award in the spring of 1953.

Except for the shortened edition of *The Journals of Lewis and Clark*, that was DeVoto's total historical career. It was a controversial career while it lasted. He publicly scorned the work of too many people to be popular. When he told the historians they couldn't write, some of them replied, No, not like you, and wouldn't want to. When he suggested that every innovation in historiography in a hundred years had been made by amateurs, he seemed to be putting down the profession that he simultaneously aspired to. When he repudiated "objective" and scientific history in favor of narrative, and especially when he chose the grand Parkmanesque subjects that the academics warned their students against, he offended some people who might have agreed with him if he had phrased his criticisms less bluntly.

 Whenever you think or hear of anything at all that happened in *1846*, DeVoto wrote his friend and mentor Garrett Mattingly in 1933, *send me a memorandum on it.* He had chosen that year as a kind of test-boring that would encapsulate the history of the frontier, and he was also looking for individuals whose careers would epitomize whole chapters of the frontier experience. He told Mattingly about one such man:

I've found a culture hero. [It was James Clyman.] Look at his career—and it's history, not my invention. Born on Washington's land in Fauquier County. Met the Gen'l in person. Down the Ohio in time to be present at Tippecanoe. Militiaman in 1812-1814. Helped Alex. Hamilton's son survey national lands in Indiana and Illinois. Got to St. Louis in time to join the 2nd Ashley expedition, which opened up the Interior basin. On the party that found South Pass. One of the four who explored Great Salt Lake in a skin boat. Five years as a fur trapper. Present at practically everything that happened in those years. Then back to Illinois, where he bought land. In Abe Lincoln's company in the Black Hawk War. Pioneered in lumber & then in farming in Wisconsin. The milksop Winnebagos shot him twice—& he'd fought Blackfeet. Got asthma & went West to cure it. To Oregon in the great 1844 emigration. In Oregon, was with the Applegate party that blazed the trail to California. Bear Flag Revolt as an associate of Fremont. Helped Hastings make his cut off, quarreled with Hastings about its safety, & denounced H's book. Met Lillburn Boggs & turned him from Cal to Oregon. Met the Donner party & advised them not to take the road they did. Met the Mormons. Came back to Wisconsin & was employed by the Mecomb party to guide them to Calif. Got to Sutter's in time to see the first gold. Married one of the Mecomb girls, bought a ranch at Napa, and lived halfway through the administration of Rutherford B. Hayes. Think that career over—and I didn't invent a comma of it.

On the other hand he could not be ignored or discredited. Nobody ever caught him in serious factual errors, however much they might object to the conclusions he drew from his facts. And many of the best Americanists respected his prodigious learning and delighted in the vigor of his prose. Not many, interrogated now, would fully subscribe to the assumptions behind DeVoto's work on the westward movement, assumptions that might be designated in shorthand as Manifest Destiny. Those assumptions, permeated with a nineteenth-century admiration for the energies of the American folk-wandering, have a jingoistic sound to the 1970's; they suggest a certain callousness toward Indians, Mexicans, and others who got in the way and were crushed. But those defects cannot be pinned on DeVoto alone. They appear in much of the history, including some of the best, of his time. The years have forced a reinterpretation that DeVoto did not live to make. Nevertheless he did the Indians the honor of learning more about them than most historians ever bothered to learn; and if he took the folk-wandering to be inevitable, he by no means condoned all its brutalities or made all its exponents heroes.

What legacy has he left to American historiography? The question should be answered by a member of the guild, not by someone who is even further outside it than DeVoto was. But it seems clear that he was one of the first to teach the profession the importance of pictorial materials such as the Miller pictures. He took the frontier of Frederick Jackson Turner's thesis and turned it into a world peopled by living men and women, a vividly realized world patiently re-created from the personal experience of those who had made it. He did something to resist the trend toward the monograph, and it is notable that many of the greatest names in the profession agreed with him on that matter of the big subject boldly grasped. One thinks of Webb, Morison, Nevins, Commager, Smith; and one remembers that though Arthur Schlesinger, Sr., objected to DeVoto's historical methods, Arthur Schlesinger, Jr., is more of DeVoto's party than his father's.

DeVoto was always challenging the shibboleths and mass judgments of the historians, as for instance he challenged the standard opinion, including that of Allan Nevins, on Frémont. But most historians would now agree that he was right and Nevins wrong, and a scorecard on his other challenges would show him with a sound batting average. No course in the history of the West can afford to leave his books off the reading list. Moreover DeVoto through his own writing and through his influence on the early years of the History Book Club had a hand in literally creating a popular taste for the real history of the West as distinguished from the sentimental, mythical, or phony.

He went to the experts and was helpless; but also he had the sense to know who the experts were. Insofar as history is an artifact, the history of the West is partly his handiwork. But no historian that I know of has adopted his dearest devices, test-boring and simultaneity, and none seems to me to be writing with a comparable narrative vigor and descriptive vividness. None that I know of has given a history book the impressionistic form of a novel. The reason may be not that historians so universally repudiate the method, but that the method is not imitable. DeVoto was sui generis. If he has a place in history, the place is among those historians who practiced an art, not a science.

*S*ure you're romantic about American history. What your professor left out of account was the fact that it is the most romantic of all histories. It began in myth and has developed through three centuries of fairy stories. Whatever the time is in America it is always, at every moment, the mad and wayward hour when the prince is finding the little foot that alone fits into the slipper of glass. It is a little hard to know what romantic means to those who use the word umbrageously. But if the mad, impossible voyage of Columbus or Cartier or La Salle or Coronado or John Ledyard is not romantic, if the stars did not dance in the sky when the Constitutional Convention met, if Atlantis has any landscape stranger or the other side of the moon any lights or colors or shapes more unearthly than the customary homespun of Lincoln and the morning coat of Jackson, well, I don't know what romance is. Ours is a story mad with the impossible, it is by chaos out of dream, it began as dream and it has continued as dream down to the last headline you read in a newspaper, and of our dreams there are two things above all others to be said, that only madmen could have dreamed them or would have dared to—and that we have shown a considerable faculty for making them come true. The simplest truth you can ever write about our history will be charged and surcharged with romanticism, and if you are afraid of the word you had better start practicing seriously on your fiddle.

Bernard DeVoto to Catherine Drinker Bowen,
Feb. 21, 1945

Wallace Stegner, the well-known novelist and editor, has adapted this essay from his biography of DeVoto, The Uneasy Chair, *to be published later this year by Doubleday & Company.*

The Burning of Chambersburg CONTINUED FROM PAGE 39

Confederate surgeon wept when he saw the flames rise and spent the morning helping victims escape. Another Confederate surgeon gave his horse to a woman to carry what belongings she could out of town. When asked who his commanding officer was, he answered, "Madam, I am ashamed to say that General McCausland is my commander!" A Confederate captain put his men to work extinguishing fires in one section of town. Another officer unbuckled his sword in disgust and left it in a Chambersburg house, where it was discovered later in the ruins.

Reactions among the townspeople varied, too. Most simply fled as fast as they could with as many belongings as they could carry to the cemetery and fields around the town, where they sat and stared unbelieving at the smoke issuing from their former homes. Others were defiant; one old woman gave a soldier such a thrashing with a broom that he hastily retreated from her house. In return for promises of amnesty a few people paid small ransoms; in some cases the promises were kept, in some cases the houses were burned anyway.

And, of course, there were those who simply added another few lines to the story of retribution. A Confederate officer, isolated from his comrades by his love for plunder, was captured by a mob of angry townspeople. Fired at and wounded, he tried to hide in the cellar of a burning house. He begged for his life, but he was shot down without mercy.

Miraculously, casualties were few during the burning of Chambersburg. Flames licked the couches of invalids, but somehow all were rescued. Children ran through the streets frightened and directionless, but in the end were reunited with their families. Damage to the town itself amounted to four hundred buildings burned, 274 of them homes, at an estimated value of about $1,500,000.

The Confederates left Chambersburg by 1 P.M. A Union officer's dispatch described their departure as "going north, taking McCausland with them drunk." Within a few hours Union troops marched through the town in pursuit, and a battle followed on August 7 at Moorefield, Virginia, during which the Confederates were badly beaten by Union soldiers shouting "Remember Chambersburg!" and "Surrender, you house-burning villains!"

Colonel Peters was never brought to trial for his insubordination. Under pressure of the Union troops' pursuit, he was released from arrest and at Moorefield went into battle again at the head of his regiment. General McCausland being absent, his second in command, General Bradley T. Johnson, ordered Peters to hold off the Union cavalry while he, Johnson, went to get support. But the Union cavalry could not be held off, and the force of the attack "carried off the Twenty-first Virginia like chaff before the whirlwind." Peters was shot through the chest; dispatches following the battle described him as "mortally wounded."

Following the battle at Moorefield, General Johnson described the demoralization of his men in his report:

It is due to myself and the cause I serve to remark on the outrageous conduct of the troops on this expedition. . . . Every crime in the catalogue of infamy has been committed. . . . At Chambersburg, while the town was in flames, a quartermaster, aided and directed by a field officer, exacted ransom of individuals for their houses, holding the torch in terror over the house until it was paid . . . the grand spectacle of a national retaliation was reduced to a miserable huckstering for greenbacks. After the order was given to burn the town of Chambersburg and before, drunken soldiers paraded the streets in every possible disguise and paraphernalia, pillaging and plundering and drunk. As the natural consequence, lawlessness in Pennsylvania and Maryland reproduced itself in Virginia. . . . Had there been less plunder there would have been more fighting at Moorefield. . . .

Whether or not General Early approved of his troops' behavior during this expedition, he never regretted his order to burn Chambersburg. In his memoirs Early wrote:

This was in strict accordance with the laws of war and was a just retaliation. I gave the order on my own responsibility. . . . It afforded me no pleasure to subject non-combatants to the rigors of war, but I felt that I had a duty to perform to the people for whose homes I was fighting and I endeavored to perform it, however disagreeable it might be.

As for Colonel Peters, despite his wound he survived, and after the war he returned to his peacetime profession as a teacher of Latin. He joined the University of Virginia faculty, and a school hall is named in his honor. Shortly before he retired in 1902, Peters' wife wrote:

The event I am proudest of in the long and useful life of my husband is that of his courageous refusal to make war on helpless women and children. . . . Too well he knew that obedience to the cruel edict of war against Chambersburg . . . would mean but a repetition of the dreadful scenes of looting, rapine and desolation that had followed the burning of Southern towns by the northern soldiery. Hence, as a Virginian, soldier and gentleman, he preferred the imminent personal risk of a violation of the command of his superior officer, to being made individually responsible for a fate so direful overtaking the defenceless inhabitants of the doomed city.

Liva Baker, a free-lance writer who makes her home in Washington, D.C., is currently working on a book on women's education in the last quarter of the nineteenth century.

Protégé of Cornwallis

CONTINUED FROM PAGE 61

Every settler in a new country labors less for the present than for the future, for himself than for his posterity, and it is this honourable consciousness that invigorates his toil, cheers his solitude, and alleviates his privations. It was not [in America] as in India, where the surplus revenue of the country was sent out of it, without being counterbalanced by any return. Here, this surplus would be expended *in* the country, whose property indeed it was, in national improvements. America was a farm, in which the produce was spent upon the land; India, one in which even stubble was carried from it.

In Baltimore, Twining thanked the other passengers for "the polite attentions they had shown me; for though a total want of reserve amongst themselves almost degenerated sometimes into coarseness, their behaviour towards me was uniformly obliging." In that city and later in Washington he spent some hours with Thomas Law, a former district governor in the Bengal civil service, who had come to America to invest a quarter of a million dollars in speculative enterprises. Law had put much of his money in the purchase of some 1,600,000 square feet of real estate in the Federal City between the waterfront and the Capitol. At the time of Twining's visit Law, who was thirty-nine, was honeymooning with nineteen-year-old Elizabeth Parke Custis, granddaughter of Martha Washington. Twining confessed that he had expected "something rather more advanced" in Washington, and he doubted that the city would ever really become the national capital or that Law would recover his investment.

The Laws asked Twining to deliver a miniature portrait of President Washington and gave him a "very flattering" letter of introduction. One of the passengers on the return journey (the son of Governor John Hancock of Massachusetts) learned of the

letter and the miniature and told the rest of the company, "upon whom it seemed to make an extraordinary impression, procuring me their congratulations on being honored with such a charge, and particular marks of their attention during the remainder of the journey."

In Baltimore again, Twining chanced to run into a distinguished foreign visitor whom he had first met when dining at the Binghams'. He was the Comte de Volney, French scholar and author, one of the first European savants to visit the Middle East beyond Greece. Volney had fled the French Revolution to take asylum in the United States. He was one of many thousands of French exiles and refugees who came in successive waves—royalists, republicans, colonials escaping from uprisings in the West Indian islands. Many came with unrealistic, even absurd, notions of life in the New World, expecting the new American man to be just, rational, and saintlike. When confronted with the realities of American conditions and character, some were disillusioned and bitter.

It appeared to me that Monsieur Volney and others who had visited this country were disappointed because they had unreasonably expected too much; and that they were unjust in blaming a state of society that could hardly be otherwise than it was. I thought it not extraordinary, much less a ground of reprehension, that the roads of America should be bad; that the stages should be called waggons and *be* nearly such; that a republican shopkeeper should receive his customer without taking off his hat or saying more than yes or no; that the English language should be spoken more fluently than correctly. In a country abounding with genius, energy and enterprise; whose infant years have produced a Washington, a Franklin, and a Jefferson; whose improvement in the most important arts of life is advancing with an impulse unexampled in the history of any

people; the imperfections inseparable from all human beginnings will gradually disappear, and often, it is not improbable, be replaced by models commanding imitation instead of sarcasm and reproach. . . .

Arriving in Philadelphia on May 11, though unwell "with a slight return of my Indian symptoms," Twining checked the condition of his animals, still grazing on Bingham's lawn, and called on Dr. Ross and other friends. He then made his visit to President Washington. The product of the meeting was a remarkable close-up look at the hero of the age.

He lived in a small red brick house on the left side of High Street, not much higher up than Fourth Street. There was nothing in the exterior of the house that denoted the rank of its possessor. Next door was a hairdresser. Having stated my object to a servant who came to the door, I was conducted up a neat but rather narrow staircase, carpeted in the middle, and was shown into a middling-sized, well-furnished drawing room on the left of the passage. . . . There was nobody in the room, but in a minute Mrs. Washington came in, when I repeated the object of my calling, and put into her hands the letter for General Washington, and his miniature. She said she would deliver them to the President, and, inviting me to sit down, retired for that purpose. She soon returned, and said the President would come presently. Mrs. Washington was a middle sized lady, rather stout; her manner extremely kind and unaffected. She sat down on the sofa, and invited me to sit by her. I spoke of the pleasant days I had passed at Washington, and of the attentions I had received from her granddaughter, Mrs. Law.

While engaged in this conversation, but with my thoughts turned to the expected arrival of the General, the door opened, and Mrs. Washington and myself rising, she said, "The President," and introduced me to him. Never did I feel more interest than at this moment, when I saw the tall, upright, venerable figure of this great man advancing towards me to take me by the hand. There was a seriousness in his manner which seemed to contribute to the impressive dignity of his person, without diminishing the confidence and ease which the benevolence of his countenance and the kindness of his address inspired. There are persons in whose appearance one looks in vain for the qualities they are known to possess, but the appearance of General Washington harmonized in a singular manner with the dignity and modesty of his public life. So completely did he look the great and good man he really was, that I felt rather respect than awe in his presence, and experienced neither the surprise nor disappointment with which a personal introduction to distinguished individuals is often accompanied.

The General, having thanked me for the picture, requested me to sit down next the fire, Mrs. Washington being on the sofa on the other side, and himself taking a chair in the middle. He now inquired about my arrival in America, my voyage, my late journey, and his granddaughters, Mrs. Law and her sister, who had accompanied me to Alexandria. He asked me my opinion of that town, and seemed pleased with the account I gave of the extraordinary activity I had observed there. In the course of the conversation I mentioned the particular regard and respect with which Lord Cornwallis always spoke of him. He received this communication in the most courteous manner, inquired about his lordship, and expressed for him much esteem. . . .

After sitting about three quarters of an hour, I rose to take my leave, when the General invited me to drink tea with him that evening. I regret to say that I declined this honor on account of some other engagement—a wrong and injudicious decision for which I have since reproached myself. No engagement should have prevented my accepting such an invitation. If forwardness on such occasions be displeasing, an excess of delicacy and reserve is scarcely less to be avoided. However, this private intercourse with one of the most unblemished characters that any country has produced had entirely satisfied me, and greatly exceeded my previous expectations, which had been limited to the usual transient introduction at a public levee. This, then, forms one of my most memorable days.

The main purpose of his visit was now realized, and Twining booked passage to England on an American ship, the *Atlantic*. Learning then that the sailing would be delayed for some days, he travelled to New York to visit a friend, Gabriel Shaw, with whom he had gone to school in England. Just beyond the Dutch town of Newark, "one of the neatest and prettiest towns I had seen," the carriage went out of control on the steep road leading down to the wooden bridge over the Passaic River. Twining jumped to safety, suffering as a result a bad cut on his right leg.

He had his wound dressed by an apothecary in New York, rented a room in a boarding house near City Hall, and went out in search of his friend, whose address he did not know. When he found the house at last, he was dismayed to learn that Shaw had just left with friends on a "foot excursion" to West Point, there to pluck a blade of grass from the grave of Major John André, executed sixteen years earlier as a British spy.

Twining rested his leg briefly and then hobbled about with a stick, inspecting the sights of New York. He visited the quays at the entrance into the East River; the fish market; the Battery and its handsome promenade; and a museum, which displayed shells and fossils, the weapons and dress of Indian tribes, and a perpetual-motion machine.

I was too lame to walk up the whole length of Broadway. I was told that it extended two miles, but as it was usual in America to reckon *as* streets such as were only *contemplated* and not yet begun, it was not easy to know how much of this great length was imaginary. Although the beauty of New York is, for the present, confined to its position, it possessing no very good street but Broadway and no pre-eminent building except the Federal Hall, it is, upon the whole, the most agreeable as well as the most flourishing city in the United States, combining the cheerfulness and commercial activity of Baltimore with the extent and population of Philadelphia.

Twining could wait no longer for his friend to return, for he feared to lose his passage on the *Atlantic*, and after a visit of four days he took the stagecoach to Philadelphia. His ship did not sail for another week, however, and in that time Shaw managed to get to Philadelphia for a visit.

So ended my successful and agreeable visit to the United States of America, a great and fine country, destined henceforth to hold a conspicuous rank amongst nations, and to take an important part in the transactions of the world. I have ever considered my decision to return this way to England as a fortunate circumstance, producing much satisfaction at the time, and a store of matter for retrospective meditation.

Thomas Twining sailed for England on May 31, 1796, and returned to India in 1798. During his second tour of duty he rose to the post of officiating judge and magistrate of Behar, and he married Mary Cock of Benares, who died in India a few years later. He resigned the service in 1806, at age thirty, for reasons of health ("the usual liver complaint") and returned to England to live a retired life. He married again and settled for a time near Northampton; begot children; rode with the famous Pytcherly hunt; bred horses, two of whom were noted jumpers; and again buried a young wife when she died of scarlet fever, caught while visiting the poor of the village. For some twenty years he lived with his children in apartments in Paris and Milan, spending his summers in Interlaken and travelling extensively about the Continent. He returned to England for good in 1837, settling in Twickenham in Perryn House, near the Thames Ferry. He became one of Her Majesty's Justices of the Peace and (in the words of his son) "disposed of no less than 970 cases up to 1847, when advanced age induced him to resign amid tokens of the highest appreciation." He died at Twickenham on Christmas Day in 1861, at age eighty-five. ☆

Only One Life, But Three Hangings

By GEORGE D. VAILL

In September a statue of Nathan Hale, martyr-patriot of the Revolution, is to be unveiled near the main entrance to the CIA headquarters in Washington. A similar statue has stood for some years next to the headquarters of the FBI, and there are other copies of it in New London and Bristol, Connecticut, and at Phillips Academy, Andover, Massachusetts. Hale was hanged by the British in New York in 1776 while on a behind-the-lines espionage mission for General Washington. It has been claimed that he was betrayed by his first cousin, a Tory —and a Harvard graduate.

In 1914 the original of this statue was erected in front of Nathan's college dormitory, Connecticut Hall, on the Old Campus at Yale, where he received his B.A. degree in 1773. Created by the noted American sculptor Bela Lyon Pratt, the stylized, slightly larger-than-life-size design was based on contemporary descriptions of Hale, of whom no portrait existed. For more than a half century the patriot stood in heroic dignity watching over the passing generations of Yale students. Then, in June of 1969, he suddenly disappeared from public view.

Leaping to the conclusion that he had been removed in order to quiet student protests against the continued display of a symbol of militarism, angry alumni and townspeople sent irate letters to university authorities and to the local press. A lady from a nearby town, having visited the campus and found the statue missing, wrote that it was "impossible NOT to attribute the 'burying' of Nathan Hale by Yale to the demonstrations & disorders at Yale against Vietnam, the draft...and the demonstrations against the ROTC." She also stated that she would "appreciate a direct, unequivocal answer" as to where Nathan was.

Two hundred years after his first hanging, Nathan Hale again impassively suffers the noose.

Author George D. Vaill (background) extracts the time capsule as the statue is trucked off.

A passing patriot stands foursquare on the vacant pedestal.

Actually, except for an occasional graffito chalked on the pedestal, the statue had generated no manifestations of protest, even in times of maximum antiwar activism. And far from being politically inspired, Nathan Hale's removal had been merely a matter of housekeeping. For a long time the statue had needed cleaning, especially since, about ten years earlier, a tinsmith working above on the eaves of the building had spilled a can of muriatic acid, a quantity of which had hit Nathan squarely on the head and given him the appearance of having had milk poured over him. Estimates had been obtained for having him cleaned, but each successive year's budget had carried too many items commanding a higher priority than Nathan's refurbishing.

In order to make a copy of the statue to stand in front of Nathan Hale House, a new dormitory at Phillips Academy, the Renaissance Art Foundry of South Norwalk, Connecticut, had borrowed Bela Pratt's original plaster model from the Lyman Allyn Museum in New London. After the new statue was made and sent to Andover, the plaster cast was destroyed in a fire at the foundry. Renaissance asked Yale for the loan of the original statue so that the model could be reconstituted for the museum. In return the foundry offered to clean and refinish the bronze.

When, in June of 1969, the men from Renaissance came to the campus to take Nathan away, they decided that the only practical way to lift him from the pedestal was to put a noose around his neck and hoist him with a power winch. After the statue was removed, I discovered a vertical hole in the center of the pedestal and in it a bronze canister. Because of water seepage and freezing, this had burst open, disclosing a pulpy, illegible mass—the remains of the papers that had been deposited

Mr. Vaill is assistant secretary of Yale University and a habitual reader of AMERICAN HERITAGE.

there when the statue was dedicated in 1914. I later found a list of these papers in the library archives.

While the statue was absent New Haven schoolboys attending summer programs on the campus amused themselves by climbing up on the pedestal and posing for passing photographers. In the meantime I had a new brass canister made and selected for it a number of contemporary items, such as newspapers, catalogues, and pictures—one of which showed Yale geologists studying Apollo 11 moon rocks, the first to reach New Haven following man's initial lunar landing. Another photograph showed Amy Solomon, a freshman, registering as the first female undergraduate student in Yale's history (she received her B.A. on June 4—exactly two hundred years after Nathan received his). Also encapsulated was a copy of the list of the contents of the original cylinder.

On September 30—the fifty-fifth anniversary of its first installation—about two hundred people gathered to see the refurbished statue rededicated. I gave a brief history of the sculpture and told of its recent travels. Then university president Kingman Brewster, Jr., dropped the new "time capsule" into the hole, and Nathan, protectively swaddled, was once again hoisted with a noose (his third hanging) and restored to his customary place of honor. Those who pass Connecticut Hall or look out through its windows can once again read Nathan Hale's legendary last words around the base of the statue: I ONLY REGRET THAT I HAVE BUT ONE LIFE TO LOSE FOR MY COUNTRY. ☆

Kingman Brewster, Jr., plants a new time capsule to replace the faulty 1914 original.
ALL THREE: BENONI J. TRUSLOW

The beleaguered martyr, nicely cleaned, is lowered into place. The toga is temporary.

At last Hale is free to resume his vigil over the Yale campus.

POSTSCRIPTS TO HISTORY

FRANKLIN AND THE BELL

The article in our June issue on the crack in the Liberty Bell ("Whose Fault Was It?") brought an interesting comment from John Hinshaw, president of the Chatham Press, which last month published a book called *Ring In the Jubilee: The Epic of America's Liberty Bell*, by Charles Michael Boland. Mr. Hinshaw observes, first of all, that the misspelling of the word "Pennsylvania" in the bell's inscription must be charged to Isaac Norris, speaker of the Assembly of the colony, who made the same error in the original order for the bell sent to London in 1751. Furthermore, according to the new book, the bell's famous motto from Leviticus was probably not chosen by Norris, a solid, unimaginative citizen, but by his good friend Benjamin Franklin—already in 1751 a notable member of the Pennsylvania Assembly. That was the year of the fiftieth anniversary of William Penn's Charter of Privileges, which, as Franklin observed in his newspaper, the *Pennsylvania Gazette,* had brought the colony a period of "vast improvement . . . Orpheus is said to have built a city by his music . . . but the sweetest of all sounds is LIBERTY; and wholesome Laws with good Government make the most enchanting HARMONY." It was also the year in which Franklin first made his radical proposal of a union of the American colonies: ". . . a voluntary Union entered into by the Colonies themselves, I think, would be preferable to one imposed by Parliament." When such ideas as these are compared with the quotation on the bell and its context in Leviticus, says Mr. Hinshaw, the likelihood of Franklin as selector of the inscription becomes

convincing, even in the absence of hard historical evidence. "And ye shall hallow the fiftieth year," Verse 10 of Leviticus 25 reads, "and *proclaim liberty throughout all the land unto all the inhabitants thereof:* it shall be a jubile unto you. . . ." (The added italics indicate the part of the quotation that appears on the bell.)

If Ben Franklin went to heaven, as he often said he hoped he would, he must have looked down with peculiar satisfaction upon the ultimate celebrity of the bell as a symbol of American independence and unity.

SAVING THE *QUEEN*

It is all too rarely that we can offer our readers truly good news about the progress of historic preservation, but some has recently come our way that we are delighted to pass on. Those who read "The Fight for the Queen" in our April, 1971, issue will recall that the majestic old sternwheeler *Delta Queen*, last of the Mississippi River packets, was in danger of being forced into premature retirement largely through the opposition of one man. The man was Edward A. Garmatz, a representative from Maryland, who presided over the House Committee on Merchant Marine and Fisheries. This committee had decided that under the stipulations of the 1966 Safety at Sea Act, the *Queen* was a deathtrap. Never mind the million-dollar improvements that made the ship as safe as

any vessel afloat; her superstructure was made of wood, and she had to go. Congressman Garmatz, apparently feeling that his prestige was being challenged, quietly pigeonholed every one of the twenty-five bills to spare the *Queen*. Finally, through some elaborate congressional sidestepping, the *Queen* was given a three-year extension, which is due to expire this November.

Does this mean that the same wearing fight will have to be waged all over again? Probably not. Garmatz has left the House, and his committee is now presided over by a true friend of the *Delta Queen*, Missouri Democrat Leonor K. Sullivan, senior woman in the House and the first of her sex to head a House committee in the past twenty years. On March 16 she introduced a bill to give the *Delta Queen* a five-year reprieve. Though the salvation of the *Queen* is still not certain, there should be far less opposition than in 1970.

Concomitant good news is that while the *Queen* is sliding up and down the Mississippi during the next two years, an elegant sister riverboat will be under construction for Greene Line Steamers, the operators of the

Delta Queen. The 379-foot vessel will be built of modern materials—no wood—and is designed to look like the old riverboats (see picture of model, opposite page). For a while it was thought that she would be propelled by gas-turbine jet engines; but in the end tradition prevailed, and the moving force will be a steam-powered stern paddle wheel. Accommodations and décor will be as de luxe as anything ever seen by Mark Twain, and the cost of the vessel—fifteen and a half million dollars—probably would stun him into total silence.

NINEVEH, TYRE, AND . . .

Those who look for parallels between the past and the present may draw some rather gloomy conclusions from this statement by Professor Gerald F. Else, director of the University of Michigan Center for Coordination of Ancient and Modern Studies. It appeared in a recent issue of *Humanities* magazine. In answer to the question "If you were a guest lecturer addressing a Political Science class, what would you say to arouse their interest in studying the Classics?" Professor Else replied:

I might say this: Once upon a time there was a young republic which had only minor interest or importance in international affairs, devoting herself instead to internal development. Then came a day when she played a leading role in the victorious effort to defeat an aggressor who was threatening the entire free world. In gratitude, the other members of the victorious coalition acknowledged her leadership, through various treaties, and she became by far the richest and most powerful state in the free world. In time, however, her management of her power alienated her friends, and the world was more and more divided between her orbit and that of the second greatest power, a former ally. Finally she allowed herself to be drawn into a war with that former ally, and in spite of her incomparably greater wealth, freedom, and technical know-how, she was defeated and never became a world power again, except for one brief period—the republic is, of course, Athens between 480 and 380 B.C.

Every generation assumes that it is the first to discover sex, and, for that matter, humor; we reprint this old wheeze as a mild corrective for any *Playboy* readers among us. (And will Amtrak please study that cozy car?)

TWO HUNDRED YEARS HENCE.

A Correspondent having favoured us with the following Picture of what he fears may be realized two hundred years hence, we submit it to the public just as we received it.

GREAT BRITAIN.	AMERICA.
LONDON—A Village supporting a few Fishermen, who make a wretched subsistence, by catching plaice, flounders, and other small fish.	PHILADELPHIA—An Imperial City, rich in all the products of the earth, and carrying on an immense commerce with half the globe.
Bristol—Ditto.	*Boston*—A large mercantile city.
Liverpool—Ditto.	*New York*—Famous for its shipping.
York—A turnip-field.	*Charles-Town, South-Carolina*—famous for its silk manufacture.
Edinburgh—A deserted rock.	*Newport; Rhode-Island*—A town famous for its fisheries.
Winchester—Formerly famous for its trade in corn—now a waise ground.	*Annapolis*—Remarkable for its amazing trade in tobacco.
Norwich—Consisting of three houses, in one of which they shew the remains of a machine for weaving stuffs.	*Reading*, in the Colony of *Massachusets* —famous for its extensive woollen manufacture.
Dover—In possession of the Prussians, who over ran France, and took this place, in the last century.	*Quebec*—A fortress commanding the whole district of *Canada*, and the adjacent countries.
Oxford— } *Cambridge*— } Of about twenty houses each : in either place is a ballad-printer's.	*New-Jersey*—A collegiate city, famous all over the world for the learning of its members.
In what WAS *London.*	In what IS *Philadelphia.*
Buckingham-house—A dunghil.	—A Palace.
Westminster-hall—A Methodist meeting-house.	—A High Court of Justice.
St. Paul's Church—A brothel.	—A Cathedral.
Guildhall—A stable.	—Grand Mews.

General Face of the *Countries.*

Barren—waste—wild—with some few remains of its ancient splendor.	Rich—flourishing—cultivated — with new cities, towns, and villas, arising on every side.

POPULATION.

Seventeen thousand.	Seventeen million.

In July, 1776, a contributor to London's *Lottery Magazine* stared into his crystal ball, with the above results. By way of explanation he probably would have cited one of those basic deteriorations in British moral fibre perennially perceived by crusty old colonels in English letters columns. Mr. Merritt Ierley, Jr., who is doing a book on the year 1776, found us this.